BTRIPP BOOKS

BOOK REVIEWS FROM

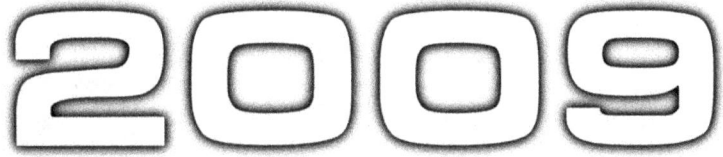
2009

BY
BRENDAN TRIPP

These reviews originally appeared on the
"BTRIPP'S BOOKS" book review blog:
http://btripp-books.livejournal.com/

Copyright © 2016 by Brendan Tripp

ISBN 978-1-57353-409-3
An Eschaton Book

Front cover photo courtesy Kenn W. Kiser via morguefile.com.
Back cover photo courtesy Sebastian Santana via morguefile.com.

PREFACE

From 1993 through 2004, I ran the *first* manifestation of Eschaton Books (now in its third revival). Initially started as a vehicle to publish my poetry, it soon became evident that the market for poetry is vanishingly small, and in 1994 we "pivoted" into being a metaphysical press.

In this time, I was largely a one-man shop, doing everything from editorial to shipping, which was a huge time commitment, and I typically worked 14 hour days, 7 days a week to keep things moving. I bring up all this here because, despite having been a life-long avid reader, during this period I had precious little time for reading, and what reading I *did* get done was largely reviewing book submissions. However, I never stopped *buying* books, which began to stack up in prodigious "to be read" piles.

When Eschaton went out of business in 2004 (in a not unusual denouement for a small press – we had a distributor who ended up never paying us, while selling through all our stock), I found myself with a lot of reading to catch up on, and a need to keep my writing chops sharp. So, I began to pen little reviews of what I was reading through, and post those on the web.

As the years went by, this became "a thing" that I was doing, and, for a while, I was targeting a fairly aggressive goal of getting at least 72 non-fiction books read per year. By 2015, this had resulted in my having read and reviewed 700 books over that 12-year span.

In recent years (since the upswing in print-on-demand publishing), I have had numerous acquaintances suggest that I put out my reviews as books. I was, at first, rather hesitant on the concept (as, after all, the material was free to read on the web), but I eventually figured that if various people thought it was a good idea, I might as well give it a shot.

While I could have started at the beginning, with the reviews from 2004, I decided that those were less representative of the whole, so opted to begin with the most recent ones.

This seventh of these collections is probably going to be the "biggest" at 81 books covered, although having a lower page count than those from later years when I got into writing longer reviews. This fact caused me to re-assess how these were being priced. I had initially figured that I'd price the books according to the number of reviews, however, at the rate I was using (25¢ each) this would have been over twenty bucks for a 220-page volume - kind of steep.

There were a couple of people who were interested in helping sell these who were encouraging me to go to a "flat rate" per volume, which I was initially resistant to. While the print-on-demand tech is wonderful, the costs are fairly high per copy, and there had to be "enough meat on the bone" to make it into the wider wholesale markets (such as when a bookstore orders in a copy), so I had to pick a cover price that would cover that, or not be able to sell through those channels.

After messing around with the numbers, I picked the rather odd $15.97 as the price … it's "sort of" numerologically derived, being both a prime number, and a part of the famed Fibonacci sequence … which is both less than what most of the books had been priced (at the quarter-per rate), and enough for even the longer page-count volumes to get into "extended distribution".

As noted in previous intros, I do not write classic reviews, but more a telling of my personal interaction with a particular book. This means that I talk about where and how I got the book, how it relates to other things I've read, what sort of reactions it triggered in me (and why), and how one can get a copy if it sounds appealing. I recently read a biography of Hunter S. Thompson, and noted some similarity in my reviewing style to how his "journalistic style" was being described … but I'm not sure I'm ready to try to assume the mantle of "Gonzo". Needless to say, if the reader is devoted to "standard" book reviewing styles, this might be an irritation … however, it does make these reviews somewhat idiosyncratic to me, resulting in a collection that is something of a "my encounters with books" sort of deal, which will, hopefully, be of interest to many readers.

- Brendan Tripp

CONTENTS

v - Preface

vii - Contents

1 - Sunday, January 4, 2009
A slightly frustrating read ...
The Jesus Papers:
Exposing the Greatest Cover-Up in History
by Michael Baigent

4 - Sunday, January 4, 2009
A quick one ...
Flatland: A Romance of Many Dimensions
by Edwin A. Abbot

6 - Sunday, January 4, 2009
One more tonight ...
Greece Before Homer:
Ancient Chronology and Mythology
by John Forsdyke

8 - Sunday, January 11, 2009
What to say?
The Wit and Wisdom of Benjamin Franklin
by Benjamin Franklin

9 - Sunday, January 11, 2009
No, really ...
Quality Management in the Nonprofit World:
Combining Compassion and Performance
to Meet Client Needs and Improve Finances
by Larry W. Kennedy

11 - Wednesday, January 14, 2009
How very strange ...
The Starseed Dialogues: Soul Searching the Universe
by Patricia Cori

13 - Monday, February 9, 2009
Not what I expected ...
The Sion Revelation: The Truth About the Guardians of Christ's Sacred Bloodline
by Lynn Picknett & Clive Prince

16 - Sunday, February 15, 2009
So, you wanna know about Buddha?
Buddha for Beginners
by Stephen T. Asma

18 - Thursday, February 19, 2009
Oooookay, then ...
Secrets of the Widow's Son: The Mysteries Surrounding the Sequel to The Da Vinci Code
by David A. Shugarts

20 - Tuesday, February 24, 2009
Memories ...
Ticket To Ride: Inside the Beatles' 1964 Tour that Changed the World
by Larry Kane

22 - Wednesday, February 25, 2009
Strange, variously ...
The Cleft and Other Odd Tales
by Gahan Wilson

24 - Wednesday, March 4, 2009
Another collection of essays ...
For This Land: Writings on Religion in America
by Vine Deloria, Jr.

26 - Saturday, March 7, 2009
Another "For Review" Book ...
The Kuan Yin Chronicles: The Myths and Prophecies of the Chinese Goddess of Compassion
by Martin Palmer

28 - Saturday, March 7, 2009
There should be much more like this ...
Home of the Brave:
Honoring the Unsung Heroes in the War on Terror
by Caspar Weinberger & Wynton C. Hall

30 - Tuesday, March 17, 2009
Not what I expected ...
The Mars Mystery: The Secret Connection
Between Earth and the Red Planet
by Graham Hancock

32 - Wednesday, March 18, 2009
More than I really needed to know ...
The Garden of Heaven: Poems of Hafiz
by Hafiz & Gertrude Bell

34 - Sunday, March 22, 2009
Important, but not essential ...
A Foreign Policy of Freedom:
Peace, Commerce, and Honest Friendship
by Ron Paul

36 - Saturday, March 28, 2009
Had we only known ...
The Vast Right-Wing Conspiracy's
Dossier on Hillary Clinton
by Amanda B. Carpenter

38 - Monday, March 30, 2009
Not quite what I was expecting ...
The Dalai Lama's Little Book of Inner Peace:
The Essential Life and Teachings
by His Holiness the Dalai Lama

40 - Saturday, April 11, 2009
Well, that was interesting ...
Without Marx or Jesus:
The New American Revolution Has Begun
by Jean-François Revel

42 - Sunday, April 12, 2009

Disappointing ...
Fight Back: Tackling Terrorism, Liddy Style
by G. Gordon Liddy

44 - Sunday, April 12, 2009

Conspiracies etc.
Secrets of the Unified Field: The Philadelphia Experiment, The Nazi Bell, and the Discarded Theory
by Joseph P. Farrell

46 - Saturday, April 18, 2009

Verrrrrry eeenteresting ... but Dated!
Competitive Intelligence: How to Gather Analyze and Use Information to Move Your Business to the Top
by Larry Kahaner

48 - Saturday, April 18, 2009

Finally - a FABULOUS book!
Masters of the Living Energy: The Mystical World of the Q'ero of Peru
by Joan Parisi Wilcox

50 - Sunday, April 19, 2009

Not his best ...
Are We Alone?: Philosophical Implications Of The Discovery Of Extraterrestrial Life
by Paul Davies

52 - Tuesday, April 21, 2009

Something interesting ...
Anasazi: Ancient People of the Rock
by David Muench & Donald G. Pike

53 - Thursday, May 21, 2009

Back to reviewing?
F5: Devastation, Survival, and the Most Violent Tornado Outbreak of the 20th Century
by Mark Levine

x   BTRIPP BOOKS - 2013

55 - Thursday, May 21, 2009

Another of these ...
Ning for Dummies
by Manny Hernandez

57 - Friday, May 22, 2009

This usually doesn't happen ...
Treasures of the Library of Congress
by Charles A Goodrum

59 - Friday, May 22, 2009

So, dat's your story, comrade? ...
The Russian Version of the Second World War: The History of the War As Taught to Soviet Schoolchildren
by Graham Lyons, Ed.

61 - Friday, May 22, 2009

A different angle on Gurdjieff ...
Views from the Real World: Early Talks Moscow, Essentuki, Tiflis, Berlin, London, Paris, New York, and Chicago as Recollected by His Pupils
by G.I. Gurdjieff

63 - Saturday, May 23, 2009

Duty ...
The Republic
by Plato

65 - Sunday, May 24, 2009

A great book ...
Religion In Practice
by Swami Prabhavananda

67 - Saturday, June 27, 2009

Another ...
Google AdSense for Dummies
by Jerri Ledford

69 - Saturday, June 27, 2009

A Classic?
The Aquarian Gospel of Jesus the Christ
by Levi H. Dowling

71 - Sunday, June 28, 2009

Hmmm ...
Understanding the Enneagram:
The Practical Guide to Personality Types
by Don Richard Riso

73 - Sunday, June 28, 2009

Wow ...
What On Earth Have I Done?:
Stories, Observations, and Affirmations
by Robert Fulghum

75 - Monday, June 29, 2009

Fascinating ...
Civilization One:
The World is Not as You Thought It Was
by Christopher Knight & Alan Butler

77 - Sunday, July 5, 2009

When is a goddess not a goddess?
The Woman with the Alabaster Jar:
Mary Magdalen and the Holy Grail
by Margaret Starbird

79 - Tuesday, July 7, 2009

More ...
The Holy Place:
Discovering the Eighth Wonder of the Ancient World
by Henry Lincoln

81 - Wednesday, July 8, 2009

Space ...
Cosmic Jackpot:
Why Our Universe Is Just Right for Life
by Paul Davies

83 - Saturday, July 11, 2009

Disappointing ...
The Path of the Pole
by Charles Hapgood

85 - Saturday, July 11, 2009

Interesting ...
The Passover Plot
by Hugh J. Schonfield

87 - Saturday, July 11, 2009

Well, the price was right ...
What About the Big Stuff?: Finding Strength and Moving Forward When the Stakes Are High
by Richard Carlson, Ph.D.

89 - Sunday, July 12, 2009

But, you've read this one already ...
The Tipping Point: How Little Things Can Make a Big Difference
by Malcolm Gladwell

91 - Sunday, July 12, 2009

A bit deeper into the stack ...
Biomimicry: Innovation Inspired by Nature
by Janine M. Benyus

93 - Monday, July 13, 2009

Puh-leeze ...
The Subversive Imagination: Artists, Society & Social Responsibility
by Carol Becker, Ed.

94 - Saturday, July 18, 2009

There's no place like home, there's no place like home ...
Love, Sex, Fear, Death: The Inside Story of The Process Church of the Final Judgment
by Timothy Wyllie

97 - Saturday, July 18, 2009

Ah ... Feynman ...
QED: The Strange Theory of Light and Matter
by Richard P. Feynman

99 - Saturday, July 18, 2009
Metaphysics by committee?
God and the Evolving Universe:
The Next Step in Personal Evolution
by James Redfield, Michael Murphy & Sylvia Timbers

101 - Monday, July 20, 2009
Great political memoir ...
Never Again: Securing America and Restoring Justice
by John Ashcroft

103 - Tuesday, July 21, 2009
A dream destroyed ...
Painting the Map Red:
The Fight to Create a Permanent Republican Majority
by Hugh Hewitt

105 - Wednesday, July 22, 2009
Brilliant ... if not for that "imaginary friend" stuff ...
Winning The Future:
A 21st Century Contract with America
by Newt Gingrich

107 - Saturday, July 25, 2009
Some amazing stuff ...
The Intention Experiment: Using Your Thoughts to Change Your Life and the World
by Lynn McTaggart

109 - Thursday, July 30, 2009
Stuff I didn't know about ...
The Jasons:
The Secret History of Science's Postwar Elite
by Ann Finkbeiner

111 - Thursday, July 30, 2009
Very odd ...
Almost Home:
A Correspondence with a Spiritual Teacher
by Kevin Edwards (Prakash)

113 - Sunday, August 2, 2009

The other ...
The Master: Parables For Enlightenment
by Kevin Edwards

115 - Tuesday, August 4, 2009

Long, long time ago ...
Civilizations of the Indus Valley and Beyond
by Sir Mortimer Wheeler

117 - Saturday, August 8, 2009

What should I be when I grow up? ...
**The Career Guide for
Creative and Unconventional People**
by Carol Eikleberry

119 - Sunday, August 9, 2009

Peer amid?
The Riddle of the Pyramids
by Kurt Mendelssohn

122 - Sunday, August 23, 2009

Great book ...
**Occult America: The Secret History of
How Mysticism Shaped Our Nation**
by Mitch Horowitz

124 - Saturday, September 5, 2009

Oddly disappointing ...
**The Presence of the Past:
Morphic Resonance and the Habits of Nature**
by Rupert Sheldrake

126 - Sunday, September 6, 2009

Some other place ...
**The Templars' Secret Island:
The Knights, The Priest, and The Treasure**
by Henry Lincoln & Erling Haagensen

128 - Friday, September 11, 2009

Help for the job hunt ...
**SHEIFGAB the World:
8 Building Blocks to Successful Job Transition**
by Conor Cunneen

131 - Saturday, September 12, 2009

Quite a treat ...
The Classic Tradition of Haiku
by Faubion Bowers

133 - Saturday, September 19, 2009

Willing to try ...
The New Science of Getting Rich
by Wallace D. Wattles

136 - Sunday, October 4, 2009

Kallisti! ...
Principia Discordia
by Gregory Hill (Malaclypse The Younger) &
Kerry Thornley (Omar Khayyam Ravenhurst)

138 - Sunday, October 4, 2009

About "what is" ...
Enchiridion
by Epictetus

140 - Sunday, October 11, 2009

Loved it, but a buck was about right ...
**Cowboy Logic: The Wit and Wisdom of Kinky Friedman
(and Some of His Friends)**
by Kinky Friedman

142 - Sunday, October 11, 2009

A mixed bag ...
Beyond Ego: Transpersonal Dimensions in Psychology
by Roger N. Walsh, M.D., Ph.D & Frances Vaughan, Ph.D

144 - Friday, October 16, 2009

Archaeological evidence of ...
**The Jesus Family Tomb:
The Discovery, the Investigation, and the Evidence
That Could Change History**
by Simcha Jacobovici & Charles Pellegrino

146 - Saturday, October 17, 2009

What to say ...
**50 Ways to Thrive, Putting the Sizzle Back Into Your
Life: A New Look at the Possibilities for Human Beings**
by Dr. Richard Talsky

148 - Saturday, October 24, 2009

Pentagrams and Golden Sections again ...
**The Sacred Geometry of Washington D.C.:
The Integrity And Power of the Original Design**
by Nicholas R. Mann

150 - Wednesday, October 28, 2009

Well ...
**Freakonomics: A Rogue Economist Explores
the Hidden Side of Everything**
by Steven D. Levitt & Stephen J. Dubner

152 - Wednesday, October 28, 2009

Quite a good read ...
Stepping Up: Make Decisions that Matter
by Timothy Dobbins

154 - Sunday, November 8, 2009

Would be nice ...
**The One Minute Millionaire:
The Enlightened Way to Wealth**
by Mark Victor Hansen & Robert G. Allen

156 - Sunday, November 22, 2009

What a bummer! ...
Brain Droppings
by George Carlin

158 - Sunday, December 6, 2009

Better ...
Napalm & Silly Putty
by George Carlin

160 - Thursday, December 10, 2009

Well, that's the third of three of these ...
When Will Jesus Bring The Pork Chops?
by George Carlin

162 - Sunday, December 13, 2009

We're doomed ...
How to Find Work in the 21st Century
by Ron McGowan

165 - Saturday, December 19, 2009

Not quite connecting ...
The Call of the Weird: Travels in American Subcultures
by Louis Theroux

167 - **QR Code Links**

189 - **Contents - Alphabetical By Author**

195 - **Contents - Alphabetical By Title**

Sunday, January 4, 2009[1]
A slightly frustrating read ...

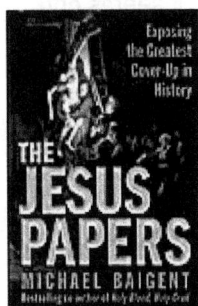

I eagerly plowed into Michael Baigent's The Jesus Papers: Exposing the Greatest Cover-Up in History[2] as an exciting start to a new year's worth of reading (yes, I have 10 other books that I haven't reviewed yet sitting here, but I felt like jumping into this one). I've been a fan of Baigent's work (individually and with collaborators such as Henry Lincoln and Richard Leigh) since the seminal *Holy Blood, Holy Grail* launched a whole "industry" of putting Christianity under various historical and mystical magnifying glasses.

Unfortunately, Baigent takes the reader on a bit of a "wild goose chase" in this book ... it *does* have a "payoff" that fits the title and general theme, but in a frustrating at-3rd-hand manner. Frankly, the book follows a pretty solid "story arc" for the first half, starting with stories of how difficult it often is to get access to obscure documents, and how they have (even after having been seen and photographed) a bad habit of disappearing behind "stonewalling" sources. The narrative then moves to the predictable South of France with the Cathars and the much-written-of Rennes le Château, discussing the brutal suppression of the former and the mysterious wealth and influence of the latter. There is (as detailed in his earlier books) a tradition that Mary Magdalene (Mrs. Jesus) at least had re-located there sometime in the mid first century, with the implication being that "hidden knowledge" persisted there about the "non-canonical" *truth* of Jesus, knowledge that the Catholic Church especially would go to extreme lengths to eliminate.

At this point the focus shifts to Israel, and looks at the context of the Biblical narrative. Baigent puts an interesting "spin" on things here that I don't recall previously seeing ... that Jesus, while being *promoted* by the Zealots as having royal/priestly bloodlines, was not particularly "in their camp", using for evidence his allowing women into his inner circle, and the whole "render unto Caesar" tax thing. There is a suggestion that the Judean Jesus was "willing to play ball" with Rome, much as the "historian" Josephus managed to do later (in switching sides from being a Zealot commander to a Roman ally). Baigent then looks around at *where* Jesus might have been over the "missing" 20 or so years of his life and settles on Egypt, where there had been a thriving Jewish community (and various schools) at the time. Much of the teachings of Jesus could come from assorted Egyptian cults, and was certainly not in lock-step with the Temple-centric orientation of his brother James and other close associates.

It's here, though, that things get "spotty". Baigent jumps from place to place and tradition to tradition to illustrate possible sources/influences on the teachings of Jesus, but without much real linkage. He even spends a *very* interesting chapter dealing with a subterranean complex in Baiae, near Naples in Italy. While this *does* sound very much like an ancient initiatory temple, and possibly the origin of the "River Styx" mythologies, it has *nothing* really to do with the Jesus story, except to nudgingly suggest that it *might* because of there having been an ancient Jewish community nearby.

Perhaps it's my personal familiarity with this sort of thing, but it seems odd to me that Baigent would spend a good third of the book just trying to *establish* that there were initiatory cults in the ancient Mediterranean! It seems a *long* way to go to be able to suggest that many of the sayings attributed to Jesus are in close relation to what has been preserved of these cults. Yes, the references that could be made to Lazarus and Mary are *fascinating*, but are ultimately only *suggestive*.

Of course, the Vatican is the big baddie in this, being the spawn of the "Greek" tradition of Paul rather than the "Jewish" tradition of James, etc. ... for the Catholic orthodoxy to have any leg to stand on, Jesus has to be a *unique* God-man whose brief tenure on Earth is the singular defining point in human history (let alone moronic modern American "evangelical" movements which need *Jeeeezus* to be GOD, complicating doctrines like trinitarianism be damned). To have solid proof that Jesus survived the crucifixion, and went on to "cause trouble" in other parts of the Roman Empire would be a Very Bad Thing for The Church of Ratzinger (and the book is recent enough to note his elevation from being the head of The Inquisition to the current Pope), the clear reason that Rome has constantly endeavored to keep things like the Dead Sea Scrolls, the Nag Hammadi library, and similar writings from the public consciousness. The Islamicists also feature in the "villain" column, as the insane attempts to assert that the Jews were *not* in Palestine for millennia have frequently led to summary destruction of any ancient buildings or document caches which offer proof of a thriving, widespread Jewish presence all over the middle east.

This point leads Baigent back into the "text trade", the shadowy underground of pilfered ancient scrolls and fragments, in which he resumes his search for "The Jesus Papers". While he is unable to back-track through his initial sources (interestingly, Catholic historians and theologians) who claim to have encountered documentation that "proves Jesus was alive in 45ce", he does, after a twisting, shrouded, and vague-on-details search get to hold in his hands a letter from 1st Century Sanhedrin court records of a *bani meshisha* ("Messiah of the Children of Israel") formally responding to accusations that he claimed to be the "Son of God", in which it's explained that he means, *filled with the spirit* of God, and not in anyway *divine*. Baigent gets to see (but not photograph) this in stabilized-atmosphere glass mountings in a room-sized safe in a European city in the presence of their owner. Needless to say, that sort of thing could change history.

Anyway, with the caveats expressed above, I highly recommend Baigent's The Jesus Papers[3] to anybody with an interest in looking behind the veil of lies which is Christianity ... it's not the book that I would have *hoped for*, but it has a whole lot of material to recommend it! The Amazon new/used guys have "like new" copies of this hardcover edition for under a buck (plus shipping), and there are "good" copies of the paperback going for as little as 1¢ ... I'm glad to have it in *my* library, and there were a good half dozen books referenced in it that I'm going to have to check out!

Notes:
1. http://btripp-books.livejournal.com/65655.html
2-3. http://amzn.to/1TfwRK8

Sunday, January 4, 2009[1]
A quick one ...

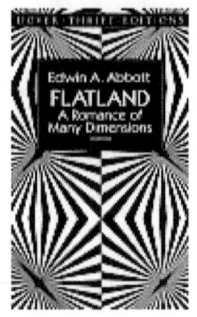

I am rather desperately behind on writing about the stuff I've been reading ... with a current back-log of 10 books. Since I seem to have hit a brick wall in *chronological* order, I'm going to "cherry pick" what seems to appeal to me to write about until I make it through this stack!

First up is Edwin A. Abbot's classic Flatland: A Romance of Many Dimensions[2]... something that you might have encountered in one of the better highschools, even though it does "fall between the cracks" between math and lit ... it's the 616th "most popular" book over at LibraryThing[3], which makes it something along the lines of 1,000 times more likely to have been read by *my* readers than the typical stuff I flog in this space. This popularity is no doubt due to the venerable nature of the book (so that one's teachers' teachers' teachers might have read it), having first been published in 1884. Abbot was a clergyman, Shakespearean scholar, and school headmaster in Victorian England who had an avocation for mathematical theory. While messing with the concepts of dimensions (such as the 11-dimension worlds of certain types of "string theory") seems mainstream to today's reader, the book was rather revolutionary in its (pre-Einstein) era, and even coupled still-challenging dimensional visualizations with cutting social commentary.

The book is "A Square" who has an encounter with a 3D-world entity (a sphere) that passes in and out of the 2D plane. In the course of the narration, the Square describes the things of his world, how social standing is determined (the number of sides, making the smooth curve of the circle presented by the sphere seem nearly divine), rules of behavior, and various hazards (the females are straight lines, being both nearly invisible and quite deadly if approached straight on).

The narrating Square has had strange dreams of one dimensional worlds, where he attempts to convince the reigning line segment of his multi-dimensional reality, and even attempts to deal with zero-dimensional point entities. These dreams seem to have been generated by the Sphere in order to give the Square some awareness of the 3D-world, which works for a time ... even too well, as the Square takes the realizations he's had of the Cube, and then begins (by extension) to query the Sphere as to 4D forms, which the Sphere stridently refuses to contemplate. When the Square tries to spread his gospel of higher dimensions, much chaos ensues, and he (and his closer associates) all end up destroyed or in prison.

Needless to say, Abbott puts together some still very challenging "thought experiments" about dimensional realities, framed within social/behavioral contexts on each level. It is, admittedly, as difficult for us to imagine 4-dimensional objects as it was for the Sphere in the story, so this book (even after 125 years) is as "fresh" on that level as the day it was written. Certainly, the "cultural" patterns detailed regarding challenging "authority" and the world-view of the masses have likewise not lost much of their value.

Flatland[4], I'm sure, is available in numerous editions. The one I have is one of those delightful "Dover Thrift Editions" which has a whopping $2.00 *cover price* (even though I picked up mine in a used book store for 50¢), so can be effectively used for one of those times when you're *almost* up to the magical $25 "free shipping" level at Amazon or B&N!

Notes:

1. http://btripp-books.livejournal.com/65857.html
2. http://amzn.to/1R2Sw6a
3. http://btripp-books.com/
4. http://amzn.to/1R2Sw6a

Sunday, January 4, 2009[1]
One more tonight ...

Just in case you're wandering in on this review from LibraryThing[2] specifically for this book and not having the benefit of the chronological unfolding of my main journal, I've gotten a bit behind on my reviews and have opted to "cherry pick" the books from the "to be reviewed" stack to deal with, this being the third I've picked up today.

Before I get into actually dealing with John Forsdyke's Greece Before Homer: Ancient Chronology and Mythology[3], I need to get one horrible half-joke out of the way ... "Unless you're George Brett, in which case it would be Pine Tar Before Homer!" ... which is a pretty clear example of why I'm not doing stand-up. Anyway ...

This is a fairly old book ... both the copy I have (which is the 1964 Norton re-print), and in general (it first came out in 1931). I found an interesting quote about the author: *"Neither a notable scholar nor an easy man to get along with, he is principally known for his war-time saving of the British Museum"*. ... it is notable that he only seems to have a hand-full of publications to his credit, despite having a rather long life (dying at age 96 in 1979). Although he lived well past Schliemann's excavations, the archaeology almost doesn't come into play here, with the focus being on what survives in the written record.

I was, frankly, amazed at how *late* it seems that writing came to the Classic world. Living in an ever-more "literate" world (made so much more so by computer communications), it's hard to imagine a culture where the knowledge is passed along by oral memory. However, the era of Homer was the early transition from the spoken to the written word, and happened only about 850bce. As such, much of the "ancient history" of the Greeks is a bit murky, and Forsdyke spends a lot of this book picking apart the various threads present in the *Odyssey*, *Iliad*, and related tales.

I suppose that, given the extreme antiquity of Mesopotamian cuneiform and Egyptian hieroglyphics (both of which were in use well over 2,000 years before "Classic" Greece), I had just *assumed* that there had been a written Greek language that had been used for all those Myths that we grow up with. Instead, this book shows, the written word came late, and many of the Myths were filled with names that were "functional" at best (translating to the equivalent of the likes of "Liar", son of "Thief") and often just made up (creating a person by back-formation of the name of a tribe or city). It is interesting to see the author "sorting through" the names to see which characters might have some historical validity among all this other "fill".

Another fascinating point is how "flexible" the Greeks were with identifying deities with those they were familiar with. Of course, coming from a culture based in part on Greco-Roman traditions, it seems *natural* for us to make the classic "substitutions", Jupiter-Zeus, Neptune-Poseidon, Pluto-Hades, Juno-Hera, Mars-Ares, Venus-Aphrodite, Mercury-Hermes, etc., and even carrying these over to other pantheons (such as the earlier Egyptian and the later Norse deities). However, it appears that if a particular God or Goddess encountered in another setting had even a passing resemblance to a Greek version, the temple, cult, or city associated with that deity would just be referred to by the name of the Greek deity, causing much confusion when trying to figure out where a particular "statue of Hermes" might be, when some very different God was actually being worshiped there. The Greeks also played "fast and loose" with foreign words, taking the name of a ruler, deity, or city and shifting it over to whatever sounded closest in Greek (a habit, I suppose, inherited by the British in their empire).

Forsdyke also spends a chunk of the book trying to sort out who might have written what, and when. This largely went "over my head" but it is supported by an interesting chart of dozens of Greek authors with their supposed dates over a 2,000 year span (from 850bce onward).

Greece Before Homer[4] appears to be out of print, but there are numerous copies of various editions available for as little as $3.99 (plus shipping) from the Amazon new/used vendors. I picked this up at a used book store last year, so there are also copies out there "free floating" if you want to go looking.

Notes:

1. http://btripp-books.livejournal.com/66239.html
2. http://btripp-books.com/
3-4. http://amzn.to/1XcWujC

Sunday, January 11, 2007 [1] Date

What to say?

This was one of those books which was obtained specifically to give me something to read on the train ride home from work when I managed to (unexpectedly) finish what I had been reading on the way up there in the morning. Fortunately, there is a used bookstore across the street from the Davis stop up in Evanston, and I was able to pop in there at lunch to find something on their "cheap" tables. I'd just finished a book[2] which was a bit Franklin-fixated, and figured that this would be a swell follow-up!

Anyway, that's how I found myself reading The Wit and Wisdom of Benjamin Franklin[3], a small, brief (under 100 pages), hardcover collection by Barnes & Noble, which didn't even bother to list who had acted as editor (although there is a 2-page Preface by an S.M. Wu and an illustrator noted).

Now, I'm not much given to reading this sort of thing, as (generally speaking) if I'm reasonably familiar with the subject of the book, I've probably gotten a smattering of its contents already, and this is hardly a selection of Franklin's "best writing". This draws from various sources, including *Poor Richard's Almanac*, and has many pages where some couplets or adages stand one or two to the page with some illustration ... none of which provide any great revelations, such as "Light Purse, Heavy Heart" or "Death takes no bribes."

I suppose that there are those out there, however, who suffer from a poor education and have no idea who Franklin is, aside from the Dead White Guy on the "benjamins". For these sorts, this might serve as a valuable introduction ... especially as it would likely also be the first exposure to the Enlightenment that they'd have (not that I'd be expecting folks to jump from this to Paine's *The Age of Reason*). I hate to suggest it as a book for *children* (as it neither flatters Franklin nor the kids), but it would be a painless read that could amuse and prove a useful basis for future reading.

Not that I'm saying the book is *bad*, it's just not very deep ... which I suppose a thin "wit and wisdom" collection isn't shooting for, and was, unexpectedly, a bit of a chore to finish (much like having to sit through a movie targeted to 8-year-olds). There was a feeling of encountering a long magazine article and skipping over the actual text and just reading the picture captions and side-bars.

If this does have some appeal to you, you're in luck, as "like new" copies are available for as little as a penny. I paid $2.00 (marked down from the $4.95 cover price), so if one was interested in adding this to one's library, I'd recommend keeping an eye out for it in the used book stores (where you'd be avoiding paying shipping)!

Notes:
1. http://btripp-books.livejournal.com/66526.html
2. http://btripp-books.livejournal.com/65409.html
3. http://amzn.to/27pyEG6

Sunday, January 11, 2009[1]

No, really ...

As I've noted previously, I've not (until very recently) been one who's been drawn to reading "business books", and this one only came into my hands (at a used book sale) due to my previous focus on getting a job in the nonprofit sector.

Frankly, one would expect Larry W. Kennedy's Quality Management in the Nonprofit World: Combining Compassion and Performance to Meet Client Needs and Improve Finances[2] (yes, that *is* its official title) would be a horrifically boring read, but it is nowhere near as dull as it sounds. Frankly, Kennedy has a reasonably lively style and an attitude which is not deadly serious and is willing, from time to time, to even poke fun at various nonprofit constituencies.

Why, you might ask, would I bother to be reading this at this point? Well, I do spend a good amount of time interfacing with the Non-Profit Commons[3] folks over in Second Life, and I figured that having this under my belt might provide me with some useful info, either in dealing with their concerns or making suggestions for programs and activities that we could jointly produce.

The author seems to have been tied into the late "quality management" guru Philip Crosby[4] (who pointed out that even for-profit organizations typically waste 35% of their resources re-doing stuff that was done wrong initially!) and takes the various elements of that approach and applies them towards the non-profit settings where he had consulted.

What makes the book *fascinating* is the string of "stories" of how things worked (or didn't) in various organizations. Rather than beat the reader over the head with points that "quality is free", or the "zero defects" concept, he identifies these and then shows how they might be attained using these illustrative scenarios.

Being the cynical person that I am, I was very drawn to his description of some non-profits ...

> (The founder) was a very emotion-centered nurturing person, and as I continued to evaluate her small staff and volunteers, I found that they were nearly clones of the founder. Each one was poorly prepared but all were emotionally committed to one another. None of them had sufficient administrative knowledge or experience, and they had little interest in such things. ... I had been asked to tell them how to get organized and secure the necessary funds for expanding their services. What I found was resistance to any real improvement or restructuring. They were not nearly as committed to meeting the requirements of their clients and constitu-

ents as they were in fulfilling their own personality needs through social action. Although their statements of purpose and individual testimonies were flowered with declarations of services to their community and the like, it was very clear that what they were gaining in their work together was more important to them personally than what their clients would receive through organizational movement.

Mighty refreshing to find that sort of honest assessment! In a similar tone he discusses the difficulties of getting a realistic and useful "mission statement" set in many of these groups (not "we want to help people" but "we want to provide X, Y, and Z services to Group A in location B"), and how to avoid "pet project" pitfalls with donors and constituents, running "fund raisers" that didn't actually produce any funds (but ego-stroke various audiences), as well as using organizational resolve in dealing with volunteers who are "off mission" and only there for the feel-good emotionalism.

Much of the advice is very "common sense" based:

> One moderate approach to achieving quality through goal-setting theory is to establish reasonable increments of improvement. A reachable target is chosen and once the goal is reached, another goal is established and so on, until the ultimate goal is reached.

Although some of it would probably be hard for the "touchy-feely" types to handle:

> The only way to improve consistently is for every person at every step in each process to try to prevent every error from reaching the client. Quality improvement will not come over-night. It will come in increments and it will be maintainable as long as you never treat an error rate as acceptable.

Given my surprising enthusiasm for Quality Management in the Nonprofit World[5], I'm rather disappointed that it appears to be currently out of print. However, "new" copies of this 1991 hardcover are available via the Amazon new/used guys for as little as $2.90 (plus shipping, of course). If you have any interest in "quality management" (or even feel like indulging in a bit of Schadenfreude over "do-gooder" types), this is quite a worthwhile read!

Notes:
1. http://btripp-books.livejournal.com/66604.html
2. http://amzn.to/1R2Ruab
3. http://nonprofitcommons.org/
4. http://www.wppl.org/wphistory/PhilipCrosby/grant.htm
5. http://amzn.to/1R2Ruab

Wednesday, January 14, 2009[1]

How very strange ...

This is another of those books that I would have been very unlikely to have picked up in a store, but when it was listed in the LibraryThing[2] "Early Reviewers" program a month back, it looked *plausible*, and (obviously) "The Algorithm" that picks who gets which book deemed me to be a good enough match to be one of the "lucky" 4.2% (356 requests for 15 copies) to get one.

I had initially understood that Patricia Cori's The Starseed Dialogues: Soul Searching the Universe[3] was another "2012" book (a subject that I have read a good deal on), and had hoped that perhaps "Starseed" had some relation to an old friend's group/center by the same name (it doesn't). I somehow missed the "channeled" aspect of this book, and (as regular readers know), I have never been particularly "open" to taking books of this sort charitably, let alone seriously.

However, there *have* been books of the genre which have surprised me, and this, at least, kept skittering around enough into areas that seemed to hold the promise of something worthwhile that it kept me from totally dismissing "The Sirian High Council" (which "speaks through" Ms. Cori in her alter ego of "Trydjya"). To be fair, much of the "skittering around" has to do with the format of this particular book, after producing a trilogy of books of this sort of material, Ms. Cori evidently had a large body of questions from her readers, clients, and participants in her various journeys, and this book is "dialogues" with the Sirians based on the questions asked by her fans. Most of the answers, unfortunately, seems like a puree of "the usual suspects", take a large dose of Zecharia Sitchin, throw in Jose Argüelles, bits and pieces of Graham Hancock, J.A. West, Robert Bauval, Charles Hapgood, James Redfield and dozens of others even less notable (heck, might as well toss in L. Ron Hubbard, as she's got critters in here that sound like Thetans, but without the jet planes), and blend until chunky, dispense as needed ... and that just explains the history and cosmology.

The "hardest to swallow" parts of this were the "ascension" concepts and the idea that beings get new DNA strands as they move up the vibrational ladder. Cori even teaches *classes* in "DNA Activation" which are "facilitated by Sirian light beings" (who I must assume have taken her advanced "DNA Facilitators Program").

Despite this sort of "woo-woo", the book does keep coming back to what, for it, seems an "even keel", the Sirians even throw a smack-down on a questioner who believed that she was "too evolved" to have to actually visit the sites being discussed, suggesting that she should *"beware of the ego"*! I did get a sense that, at heart, the book was very genuinely felt, and that it ultimately was an expression (no matter *how* over-the-edge) of sincere hope for the race. There were also a few aspects that I found surprising, as they dovetailed with materials that I've read (or worked with) in other contexts. The general concept of "vibration" (if decoupled from the whole DNA issue) is very similar to certain Shamanic teachings, and the way she described the "planetary system ascension" (of "Ra") evoked many of the implicit patterns of Richard C. Hoagland's materials on Hyperdimensional Physics, to the extent that I began to wonder if she actually *had something* there.

There was also a very deep streak of "paranoia" running though the book, manifesting in a total distrust for governments, corporations, and churches (especially Rome's). While a certain degree of watchfulness over these sorts of entities is good policy, this ran to the whole "secret world government" sort of thing where vast conspiracies managed to keep close control over thousands of participants without any substantive information ever getting out. Oh, and these groups were being run by alien-human hybrids from a "lost" planet which was in a strange orbit around both the Sirian system and the Sun (with a distance of 8.6 *light years*, that must make for one *looooooong* round-trip).

One thing you can say about The Starseed Dialogues[4] is that it doesn't leave much out. Nearly every "new age" hot-button is pushed, and it's all (more or less) woven together into a one-size-fits-all explanatory whole. If your tastes run toward the "fruit and nuts" end of the spiritual spectrum, then this book's for you. For the rest of us, well, if Cori's fans stay busy writing her and her Sirian friends, then they're just that much less likely to freak us out by having discussions with the displays in the produce section when we're grocery shopping! Were you dying to get a copy, Amazon says this is due out February 17th, and will be $16.95 retail ($11.53 at their discounted price) and they're taking pre-orders now.

Notes:

1. http://btripp-books.livejournal.com/66970.html
2. http://btripp-books.com/
3-4. http://amzn.to/1XcUIPv

Monday, February 9, 2009[1]

Not what I expected ...

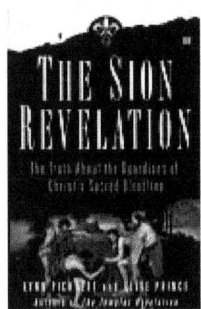

Sometimes I hit a book and find that it wasn't anything like I expected. Sometimes this manifests as a deep disappointment, sometimes as a "hidden gem", and sometimes as a "whodathunk?" eye-opener. Lynn Picknett and Clive Prince's The Sion Revelation: The Truth About the Guardians of Christ's Sacred Bloodline[2] is one of the latter sort.

Over the years, I've read quite a bit in the "Sion" genre, from the Baigent/Leigh/Lincoln books through various things inspired by them, and similar efforts. Each has had its appeal, if putting in pieces which don't quite all fit together to solve the puzzle. I had expected that The Sion Revelation[3] was going to be yet another of these, adding on a few new pieces of information, but staying within the whole "Jesus/Magdalene" nexus of the previous books.

I was surprised to find, that while the authors' research *began* there, it fairly quickly led off into quite different directions. In fact, the subtitle "The Truth About the Guardians of Christ's Sacred Bloodline", in the context of the book, is very misleading, except in the sense that the whole Priory of Sion "project" appears to *not be* about those things at all!

The book is divided into two sections, "Illusion" and "Reality". In the first section they pick apart the threads of the mythos that has arisen since *Holy Blood, Holy Grail* and see what lies behind both the popular story line, and the root materials. They look in detail at the questions of Rennes-le-Château and Abbé Saunière, and, while never quite "solving" the question of the vast wealth that came in and out of his hands, do tie the Abbé in with members of the Hapsburg line, as well as a number of "secret societies". A close look is also given to the history of Pierre Plantard, the prime source for information on the Priory of Sion. Much of what was put out in the name of the Priory was very much in line with Plantard's earlier work with the French Resistance, and other ventures such as the Alpha Galates Order, of which he was figurehead back in the 1930's (he was nominally "Grand Master", but at age 22 the odds were better that he was the "mouthpiece" for communicating their message). At one point the book "felt" like it was veering off on an extended tangent, looking at the politics of France over a century or so, but this eventually integrated with the main thrust of the story.

The essential "truth" the authors are proposing here is rather convoluted, but essentially goes like this: Pierre Plantard and his immediate associates "invent" the Priory of Sion in the 50's or 60's, essentially continuing programs that they had in place as part of the Resistance in WW2 and previously with Alpha Galates. The whole "Merovingian" and "Bloodline of Christ" story is a ruse woven in to throw folks off the "real" trail. This is not to say that Plantard, and his predecessors were *not* involved with "Secret Societies", just that they weren't involved specifically with the types that one typically associates with them.

The "true" stream leading up to the Priory appears to have begun with a Saint-Yves d'Alveydre, an 18th century occultist who merged *his* predecessors' mystical work with a political philosophy which then became known as *Synarchy*. The Synarchy concept was carried forward by an entire web of secret societies, most formed on the "chain" model (where you only knew the one person who brought you in), which makes these very difficult to trace, but it appears that many of the "modern" people on the Priory's lists of leaders had at least *some* connection to these groups (and, as the authors point out, several of the later names on the lists were prominent when they came out and yet never sued about their names appearing on those lists). Anyway, there was certainly enough "occult material" in circulation in the Synarchy line to provide Plantard & co. with all the enticing "inside information" they'd need to seed the "front" materials that they were leaking via their *"Dossiers Secret"*.

What is chilling, however, about the whole Synarchy concept, is not its *occult* manifestation, but its *political* goals ...

> *Each state must be highly organized at every level, with everyone in his or her own specific place ... Challenging one's status would not be tolerated ... the concept that everyone has a preordained place and role means that some people are naturally intended to lead: in other worlds, Saint-Yves advocated government by a predestine elite ... at its core it is an essentially spiritual or mystical philosophy. The elite is spiritually attuned to the universal laws - effectively a priesthood. Synarchy is therefore a form of theocracy...*

This would, perhaps, just be another bit of random utopianism if it wasn't for the fact (or very strong suggestion) that *all* the major players behind a "United Europe" were involved in various Synarchic groups. The book weaves together the mystical/occult groups with the frequently over-lapping *political* organizations, and suggests that what Plantard and his associates were up to was not "restoring a sacred bloodline", but installing a new sort of government structure, one that looks a whole lot like things we're seeing today.

> *After Saint-Yves's death, synarchy developed in ways that would not necessarily have met with his approval ... Revolution was out, elitist ideologies being largely unsuited to mass movement, and with the rising popularity of democracy and the concept of individual liberty it became increasingly futile to attempt to win people over by debate to the notion of a fixed hierarchy - especially as by definition most people would find themselves in the lower orders. Synarchists therefore turned to cunning, seizing power from within by infiltration. Their only hope of success lay in taking control of the institutions of government ...*

I'm surprised that I had never heard of this book from my associates in the Political Right-Wing, as what is dealt with in here certainly *explains a lot* about the actions of "The Left" over the past 50 year or so, and it certainly provides a "grand conspiracy" of the sort that the likes of Dick Hoagland tends to postulate, and it also frames a "philosophical basis" that would put some logic behind the otherwise inexplicable "anti-Americanism" that is rampant even among our own government.

I would *highly* recommend this book to anybody who "cares about America", as it seems to be the final "Revelation" that pulls the veil away from the destruction of what we traditionally have been, and what we have stood for. I wasn't *expecting* a political read when I picked this book up, but I'm certainly glad that I encountered it. What if "institutional Marxism" (in the Press, Academia, and the Entertainment Media) is just the same sort of front for an organized Synarchic push in America? The concept certainly puts a lot of the *"why would they want to do that?"* questions in a new light!

Anyway, The Sion Revelation[4] is still in print, so you could find it at your local brick-and-mortar book vendor, and "like new" copies can be had from the Amazon new/used vendors for under a buck (before shipping). This is one that I highly recommend folks pick up ... if the authors are right, their work explains a lot!

Notes:

1. http://btripp-books.livejournal.com/67093.html
2-4. http://amzn.to/1XcTFit

Sunday, February 15, 2009[1]

So, you wanna know about Buddha?

This book came in as a nice surprise. As I've noted, I'm part of the LibraryThing[2] "Early Reviewers" program, which every now and again sends me something for my review. This, however, came from a post on the E.R. boards there, and e-mail follow-up, from a contact at Hampton Roads Publishing (http://hrpub.com), who must have considered the fairly substantial part of my library that Buddhist books represent in selecting me for a review copy.

While I understood that Stephen T. Asma had *illustrated* his Buddha for Beginners[3], I wasn't quite prepared for how much of a "picture book" this is, as its content likely runs something like ¾ the author's drawings and only about ¼ the actual text ... meaning that this is, by any measure, a fast read.

This presented a bit of a challenge to me. I'm no fan of the "graphic novel" genre, and my first guess for an excessively-illustrated book is that it's shooting for a less-than-prime intellectual market. A few pages into this, I was thinking that maybe I should pass it along to my 13-year-old daughter who has "helped" me with some YA-oriented reviews, but the deeper I got into it, I realized that it really *wasn't* intended as a "kids' book" either. What *is* the market for this? It's not a children's primer, but it is "sugar coated" with extensive illustrations, yet at the same time not "dumbed down" as you might expect for either the comic book crowd or as a "gentle" approach to the Christian masses. In fact, one of the most "difficult" parts of the book is the author's attempts to condense substantial philosophical issues from Buddhism into a paragraph and a series of graphic panels. The more I tried to wrap my head around it, the more it reminded me of a long-format Chick tract (but without the hatred and, of course, the Bible-thumping), having about the same level of intense, but abbreviated, engagement with the materials covered.

Naturally, as a downside of my having studied Buddhism, I found that it was difficult for me to "blank slate" my mind to approximate a person picking this up for an initial introduction to the Buddha. In fact, most of the book served to provide flashbacks to Thich Nhat Hanh's *Old Path White Clouds* which is also something of an introduction to the Buddha, only minimally illustrated and nearly 20 times as long! In our short-attention-span world, however, *Buddha for Beginners* certainly has a leg up for the "quick investigation" of the subject!

I get the impression that the author here has a strong Hinayana bias, and he unfortunately chooses to wield it against other developments of Buddhism. Being that most of *my* direct contact with Buddhism has been of the Vajrayana variety (with lesser work with Mahayana traditions), I bristled a bit at his near-dismissals of these later forms. I suppose, in this sense, the parallels to Jack Chick (who is always happy to flail away at anybody not of his particular stripe of lock-step fundamentalism) are more to the point.

This is not to say that I *disliked* the book as a whole ... just that I found it hard to either take it on its own terms, or to classify it as "good for a particular audience". One does have to applaud the author's efforts to condense down the life and teaching of the historical Buddha into something that has both proportional breadth and depth to its length, which is quite impressive, but the above caveats keep coming to the fore. I suppose that this would work for high school students who are lacking exposure to religion/philosophy classes, as this might well spur them to further investigations, giving them just enough lingering questions, but it seems out-of-synch with (my perceptions of) "general audiences" much older or younger.

However, as mentioned above, Buddha for Beginners[4] is a fast read, and very reasonably priced. In fact, both the publisher and Amazon have it at substantial discounts. Obviously, the issues I've had with the book are not those that the vast majority of readers would likely have with it, so I'm sure that most folks picking this up would find it an enjoyable, informative, amusing, and low-time-investment read!

Notes:

1. http://btripp-books.livejournal.com/67458.html
2. http://btripp-books.com/
3-4. http://amzn.to/1spKLDj

Thursday, February 19, 2009[1]

Oooookay, then ...

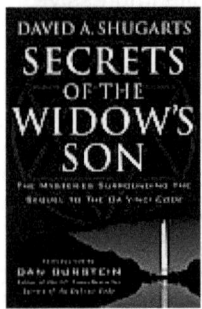

As regular readers of this space will no doubt be tempted to remind me, I am frequently of the opinion that something I've read is "strange". Many would argue that my reading habits are themselves strange, so what should I expect! However, there are times where one just ends up scratching one's head over a book, not in a "how did *this* get published?" way, or some deep metaphysical way, just in a "huh?" zone of sorts, and this is one of those.

David A. Shugarts' Secrets of the Widow's Son: The Mysteries Surrounding the Sequel to The Da Vinci Code[2] was a recent dollar store discovery, so at least the price was right. This book has a very odd purpose, it's written to sort of *predict* (back in 2005) what Dan Brown would be writing about in the sequel to his *The Da Vinci Code*, a book that appears to still be in the works.

Now, I've not read *The Da Vinci Code* nor seen the movie, but over the years I've read a good deal of the "source material", so this looked like it might be an interesting read. I guess the rumors were/are that the next book was going to take place in Washington, DC, and deal with Masons and Templars and treasure, etc., ground much trampled over by the *National Treasure* movies (one of the factors suggested for the delay, even four years ago, of the new book was that a lot of the "mythos" got used up by those). The author had been a contributor to a couple of *"Secrets of ..."* books that looked at the earlier Dan Brown books, and either analyzed some the action/background or (in Shurarts' case, having been an Aviation writer) pointed out certain technical "issues" in them. I guess when the new book was delayed, the folks behind these "Secrets of" books decided that they'd just go ahead and put out a "dig behind the story" book before there *was* a story!

Since I've not been "in on the story", I guess I've missed the "fun" of poking through the marketing ephemera of the Dan Brown industry, but it appears that he likes to hide codes in things, and somewhere in the dust cover for the DaVinci Code book there is a hidden phrase of *"Oh Lord, My God, is there no help for the widow's son?"*, a famous Masonic recognition call ... which seems to have determined for Shugarts and his editors that the new Brown book is going to be "about" the Masons.

I very rarely actually look at the reviews of a book before I read it, but I noticed that over on Amazon this book got a LOT of very negative feedback, most of it seeming to come from Masons (or, perhaps, PR shills *posing* as Masons), which made me think *"hmmm ... wonder why they're so pissed?"*. Frankly most of the savaging given the book is *way* out of proportion to anything *in* the book, which makes me think those are "misdirection" marketing ploys!

Reading this, I vacillated between a certain pity for the author's task of trying to *guess* what an upcoming book is going to be about, and then flesh out a book of his own based on those guesses, and being very irritated by the "fanboy" aspects of his writing (Dan Brown does *this*, Dan Brown does *that*, "sqeee!"). Really, I can't imagine very many people give a *damn* that his wife is a distant relative of George Washington, and peppering references to "Cousin George" through the book is just *irritating*; plus mocking *others'* flights of fancy in the midst of one's own blithering is just *bad form*.

Of course, this is not to say that the book wasn't *chock full* of "interesting" bits of information. I don't believe I'd ever read about Albert Pike previously, and the story there (albeit spun out repeatedly in side-bars to various threads being followed) was quite enticing. He also makes a half-hearted pitch to link the Mormons with the Masons, and points out some rather damaging background on the formation of the LDS Church. Heck, even "Dolly the Sheep" makes an appearance, having being cloned in Roslin, Scotland, right over by Rosslyn Chapel and Roslin Castle, ancestral seat of the noted Sinclair family!

Needless to say, I'm not making a whole-hearted recommendation on this one ... it's got enough stuff in it to make it worth the read, but I sure wouldn't want to pay retail for it! As noted, I found this at the *dollar store*, and you can get "like new" copies from the Amazon used guys for as little as a penny (plus shipping). It certainly is a strange "meta book" sort of project, but if you're into the whole "code" thing, you'll probably want to add this to your mix of conspiracy fodder!

Notes:

1. http://btripp-books.livejournal.com/67724.html
2. http://amzn.to/1qm1Hst

Tuesday, February 24, 2009[1]

Memories ...

Sometimes you can tell why a book ended up at the dollar store, and sometimes it's totally inexplicable. Larry Kane's Ticket To Ride: Inside the Beatles' 1964 Tour that Changed the World[2] is one of the latter. A fascinating window into Beatlemania, it even is "multi-media", coming with a CD of interviews done with the band when the author was part of the traveling press pool on the '64 and '65 American tours.

The only thing I can identify that might have moved this into those channels is that it was, perhaps, written too late. Forty years is a LONG time to "sit on a story", memories dim, contexts shift, and time grinds on, leaving fewer and fewer people that really care about a subject available to buy the book. Had Kane written this in '67 or '68 it would have been *huge*, and given him a life-long income of doing convention and personal appearances, so waiting till 2003 to tell this story just seems odd, like there was some hard-bargained "embargo" in place on him opening up about his experiences with the band.

Folks under 40 probably don't really understand what a major cultural force The Beatles were. Frankly, it almost sounds *silly* saying that today, but it's true. Especially for "popular music", nobody had ever toured like that, and in several instances (most notably the famed Shea Stadium show) no musical event had *ever* drawn such crowds (and that at 55,000 attendees, compared to the six-figure gates that will regularly be scheduled on major tours today). Four guys in their early 20's had the entire world's attention, and it was at a sociological point where "something different" was being ushered in.

The back story here is somewhat amusing. Larry Kane was a "serious news guy", and a news director at a Miami radio station at age 21, who by way of a few near-accidental connections was invited to come along on the '64 tour. He wasn't a Beatles fan, he wasn't "in the music business" (although his employers in radio were), and he was able to pull together an ad-hoc "network" of a few dozen stations for whom he was providing daily reports (thereby being able to finance the trip). Kane went on to have a long and reasonably distinguished news career, and maybe, for the most of that, he didn't *want* to be "The Beatles' reporter guy" and ducked the connection as much as possible.

Anyway, Kane apparently did keep his notes (and some of his reels) and it's a nice thing for a geezer like myself to be able to take a peek into that world. I was a little kid when the events in this book were unfolding, but because of my age (I'd have been like 6-8 over most of the time), The Beatles were a major "environmental" factor (especially as we were living in NYC at the time) for me growing up.

The book has no particular axes to grind, nor any specific theme. It follows the tours, city to city, show to show, and presents the events from a newsman's angle ... what happened, who was involved, etc., without any "fan" spin. This could be a bit dry for some, but it is, as noted, like getting a chance to be "a fly on the wall" for those tours. Things were so different 45 years ago, and this offers reminders, page after page, of how things used to be.

The music is almost a side issue here, only one or two glimpses are provided of new (later hit) songs being worked on (in the back of the plane), and the set list (for a remarkably short half-hour show) didn't seem to change much. Most of the venues that they were booked into at the time had less-than-adequate sound systems (and this is in a pre-stereo era!), and there is some discussion of how little the concerts were actually *heard* between the weak PA and the screaming fans.

One thing that makes "old Beatles fans" a bit wistful here is the stories of how their management made a point to keep them from being recorded. As a result, there is so very little video/film of The Beatles (except, of course, the actual *movies* that they made) performing. There's official video from Shea Stadium, and a live concert recording from the Hollywood Bowl, but not much else, meaning that as the years roll on, more and more of the awesomeness of The Beatles will fade down the "memory hole", without those culturally-preserving ephemeral traces to hold their rightful place.

Ticket To Ride[3] is a treat for any Beatles fan, and should also not be missed by "modern culture" readers either. As noted, I got this at the dollar store, so it's currently kicking around in those channels, and the Amazon new/used vendors had "like new" copies for as little as 1¢ (plus the $3.99 shipping). But, hey, what would you pay for a CD full of Beatles interviews by itself? It appears to still be in print (both Amazon and B&N have it listed), which adds to the head-scratching as to why it was at the dollar store ... so if you're interested, you should be able to find a copy.

Notes:

1. http://btripp-books.livejournal.com/68025.html

2-3. http://amzn.to/1qm1iX7

Wednesday, February 25, 2009[1]

Strange, variously ...

I mentioned picking up Gahan Wilson's The Cleft and Other Odd Tales[2] a month or so back in my main journal. This was an odd purchase made possible by my dropping my 5-year "ban" on reading fiction (having made my target of reading at least 72 non-fiction books per year in '06, '07, and '08), it was also notable as being a "road" purchase from the famed *Book Loft* in the German Village area of The Wife's hometown of Columbus, OH. The reason, however, that it was discussed prior to reading was that I'd discovered that it was significantly mis-printed, with its initial 32-page "signature" having been replaced by a copy of the 2nd 32-page section, thereby explaining why this was sitting out on the Clearance tables. I bring this up now both to note that I didn't end up reading the *whole* book (the title story being one of the missing), but also to point out that I'm hardly the *only one* with this problem ... as, if you go to the Amazon page[3] for this, you will find that the "First Sentence" quote is the initial line from p.33, meaning that the "official Amazon version" has the same manufacturing defect as my copy! This almost makes up for my missing that first part of the book.

Now, prior to encountering this book, I was unaware that Gahan Wilson was a writer. I was certainly familiar with his twisted illustrations for various well-known national magazines (among them *The New Yorker* and *Playboy*), so there was an immediate assumption that this book was likely to be long-form versions of the macabre humor he infuses his cartoons with. This was not far from the truth.

I must admit to feeling a bit awkward with discussing *fiction*, having steered clear of it for such a long period. Wilson has an interesting approach, however, which is not unlike the "window on a moment" that is a standard of his better known works. There are few tales here with much of any "context" or "backstory" provided; they start at a point and run forward with the strangeness and light horror building without getting into the details of how things came to be how they are within the telling. Most notable of this approach is a story of a fellow with a traveling "carnival" of sorts, but this carnival exists, as it turns out, simply to lure hoards of zombies to their destruction at every stop along the way. There's *zero* explanation of *how* the rural backroads of Kansas became so Zombie-infested (like, it would appear, pretty much everywhere else), just how the protagonist manages their enticement and elimination, before moving on to the next region.

In many of these stories, common items are simply not the way they are in the world *outside* the story, but exist in a world where they're the only thing amiss; among these: cats, birds, and assorted plants. There's even one in here that I *wish* somebody would option to make a twisted movie out of, a bizarre little tale called *Hansel and Grettel*, but which bears only the slightest similarity to the classic dark fairy tale.

Again, these stories exist in their own little bubbles of reality, and leave the reader with a whole raft of questions at the end of most, leaving no explanation of a multi-specied Mars, a fiction character who conquers both his author and *his* editor to achieve an existence beyond the pages of his book, and various forms of the ill-mannered dead.

This does seem to be out of print at the moment, yet seems to have a certain popularity, as the used versions of this paperback edition aren't particularly cheap. Your best bet is probably a used copy of the hardcover, which will set you back around $2.60 (plus shipping) for a "very good" copy. If this style of lucid, humorous, macabre writing appeals to you, I'm sure you wouldn't regret the read!

Notes:

1. http://btripp-books.livejournal.com/68159.html

2-3. http://amzn.to/1OtpfHj

Wednesday, March 4, 2009[1]

Another collection of essays ...

One of these days, I'll have to pick up a copy of Vine Deloria, Jr.'s *Custer Died For Your Sins*, as it seems to be the only long-format book by him. *For This Land: Writings on Religion in America*[2], like most of what I've read of Vine Deloria Jr., is a collection of essays from a rather extensive span of time (1965-1998). While this does have its advantages (it "opens a window" onto various episodes that he was involved in over those thirty-some years), it lacks a cohesiveness that would, hopefully, lend persuasiveness to one long *statement* on a subject.

Needless to say, a book of "Writings on Religion in America" from a Native perspective has a long and ugly history on which to draw, so it really *shouldn't* matter that the 30 essays collected here jump from the 70's to the 90's, back to the 60's, with brief stops in the 80's, but as the subject matter is often "topical" to the time of writing, there *is* a certain level of disjointedness that is always in the background.

This was edited by a James Treat (whose own essays set up the various sections), who grouped Deloria's writings into five areas: White Church, Red Power; Liberating Theology; Worldviews in Collision; Habits of the State; and Old Ways in a New World. It is amusing to see the difference between the populist writer Deloria and the academic writer Treat, as the pace of the book bogs down every time one hits one of the introductory segments!

Vine Deloria Jr. was a fascinating figure, active without being an "activist" particularly, from a "Christianized" native family (and being a seminary graduate) but rejecting that for a search for his cultural roots, a lawyer whose writing would never suggest that craft, and widely read on many subjects. Every book I've read of his opens my eyes to some new factoids that I had not previously encountered (I believe that I am *especially* grateful for his introducing me to *Without Marx of Jesus* a book from the early 70's, a used copy of which I'm eager awaiting the arrival of).

One of the other things that I found *fascinating* in here was a story of how White Liberalism turns everything it touches *bad*, specifically in the case of the Episcopalian Church in the late 60's. Now, I grew up Episcopalian (my father had been a minister), and I saw much of the insanity that Deloria writes about from a completely different side, with the eyes of a 10-16 year-old. The GCSP that he writes about here was a six-year "hijacking" of one of the major Protestant churches by left-wing radicals over a rather turbulent time ('67-'73). One would expect that there would be sufficient "institutional inertia" in an organization like the Episcopalian Church to fend off this sort of thing, but whole internal groups were, in a matter of months, Stalinistically "purged" of non-radicals and substantial chunks of the organizational budget were put at their disposal (this could go a long way to explaining how my childhood church ended up as a rallying point and "dorm" for the rioters at the '68 Democratic Convention).

Anyway, as interesting as that was to me personally, it's hardly the main focus of the book ... predictably, this focuses on how Christianity, primarily through deceit and down the barrel of a gun, bullied its way across America. There are certainly other subjects in here (his discussions of "sacred lands" and how these are *essential* to the Native religion yet not even on the radar of the Christians are particularly clarifying), but the unseeing / unfeeling / uncaring Christian onslaught is never far from view.

Deloria does paint a bit of a hopeful picture of a "post-Christian" America, where the Native ways (he notes how even White settlers, once they've been in the same place for four or five generations, start acting more like Natives) will reassert themselves, absorb whatever isn't toxic from Christianity, and have the wheel turn.

While For This Land[3] was not as engaging to me as some of his other books have been, it was still interesting enough, and a worth-while read. This is still in print, but with a rather steep ($32.95 for a 320-page paperback) cover price, so you might consider the used channels, where a "Very Good" copy can be had for around three bucks, were you inclined to add this to your library as well.

Notes:

1. http://btripp-books.livejournal.com/68514.html

2-3. http://amzn.to/27p8Jyv

Saturday, March 7, 2009[1]

Another "For Review" Book ...

I was pleasantly surprised to get this in the mail last week from Hampton Roads Publishing (http://hrpub.com), the group that had contacted me via LibraryThing[2] to see if I'd be interested in reviewing some titles outside of LT's "early reviewer" program. I guess they weren't overly upset by my less-than-rave review[3] of Buddha for Beginners.

Unfortunately, I find many of the same caveats in The Kuan Yin Chronicles: The Myths and Prophecies of the Chinese Goddess of Compassion[4] by Martin Palmer (with Jay Ramsay, poet, and Man-Ho Kwok, translator). It's almost as if there was an institutional (I know, I'm only judging from *two* books) "anti-Shamanic" bias over there that serves to marginalize (or even outright ignore) traditions with strong Shamanic elements. At least in this book the Tibetan Goddess Tara is *mentioned*, but in being a female expression of Avalokitesvara (same as Kuan Yin), you'd think she'd rate as much ink as the Japanese Kannon, but Tara doesn't even make it into the Index.

Frankly, I got "faked out" by the sub-title here: "The Myths and Prophesies of the Chinese Goddess of Compassion", and was sort of expecting more of a collection of bits and pieces presented pretty much on their own. This is *not* the case. If fact, the first *third* of the book is a historical look at Kuan Yin in China. the second third a discussion and "modern re-telling" of various "Myths & Legends" about Kuan Yin, and the last third an analysis of the "Poems of Kuan Yin", which are used (much like the I Ching) for divination, along with a new translation.

There are some fascinating bits in the fist section, of how the figure of Avalokitesvara (a male bodhisattva) evolved into the *female* figure of Kuan Yin (again, as happened in Tibet with the manifestation of Tara). One of the factors the authors cite is the presence of Christian missionaries in China, bringing icons of Mary, which (they suggest) served as a template for the eventual representations of Kuan Yin. Another note of interest is that "Kuan Yin" is a shortened version of her original Chinese name, Kuan Shi Yin ...

> She is normally only known as Kuan Yin. This is because in the mid-seventh century, it became a capital offense to utter the word "shi". This was because it formed part of the original name of the founder of the Tang dynasty, Li Shi Ning. Eager to forget his poverty-stricken and working-class origins, mention of his original name was banned on penalty of death.

... quite an incentive for a name change!

The "Myths & Legends" section discusses the development of the cult of Kuan Yin through various stories from different areas. These are re-told in a rather conversational way, which would be interesting to see in parallel with a more "linear" translation.

Finally, there is the divinatory aspect where 100 poems (in the original, these have the same format, four lines of seven characters each, the translator opted to go for the "meaning" and let go the formal structure) were used as the answer to a question posed while shaking a container with 100 numbered sticks ... the stick that first fell out was the poem you were supposed to read.

The Kuan Yin Chronicles[5] is an interesting book, it has history, analysis, divination, and just enough devotion to make it seem heart-felt (I, personally, would have preferred to have had more of the latter in the forms of some specific Kuan Yin meditations). It has just been released, and both Amazon and the publisher[6] have it at a discount. If you've ever wondered about Kuan Yin (I grew up with a statue of her in our back-yard garden, and this would have been a handy book to have read back then), this will certainly familiarize you with her!

Notes:

1. http://btripp-books.livejournal.com/68735.html

2. http://btripp-books.com/

3. http://btripp-books.livejournal.com/67458.html

4-5. http://amzn.to/27p7UWm

6. http://www.hamptonroadspub.com/book/562

Saturday, March 7, 2009[1]

There should be much more like this ...

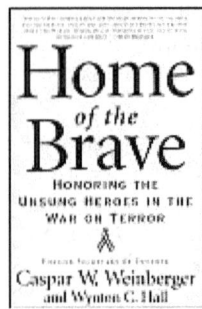

Home of the Brave: Honoring the Unsung Heroes in the War on Terror[2] is a book of tributes to a selection of U.S. military heroes who have fought in Afghanistan and Iraq. Assembled by Caspar Weinberger (Secretary of Defense in the Reagan administration), and penned by speechwriter Wynton C. Hall, this is a celebration of the heroism of our troops in the field ... the sort of stories that in previous generations would have been on the front page of the newspaper, or made into laudatory movies.

... after years of watching and reading coverage of the War on Terror, many citizens, including us, have been awestruck by the lack of balance and objectivity exercised by many American reporters an new executives. The dearth of hopeful or heroic stories reported has given viewers a lopsided perspective. It seems that many in the media are wiling to highlight only the actions of service members who can be portrayed as either victims or villains.

It's a damning realization that most of these men and women's stories are *unknown*. The Mass Media had become so solidly anti-American since Viet Nam that the ONLY news that gets reported is that which makes us look bad. Weinberger wanted to make a stand against that, and put together this volume.

The tales of 19 members of our armed services are related here, recipients of the Navy Cross, the Silver Star, Distinguished Service Medal, and even the Medal of Honor. Some of these heroes gave their lives in their actions, some are still (at the time of writing, 2006) serving, and some have rejoined civilian life. One of these is a woman, the first female GI ever awarded the Silver Star for active combat. Another, a Mexican immigrant, joined the Marines the day he received his green card and went on to make the ultimate sacrifice, mortally wounded, he covered an enemy grenade with his body to save his squad.

These stories are told from a boots-on-the-ground standpoint, as though you were walking patrol with these soldiers. Weinberger (and Hall) do a masterful job of putting the reader in the action, while putting the action within the context of the struggle.

For *anybody* who is not part of the "blame America first" cabal, Home of the Brave[3] will be encouraging reading, if frequently emotional. I am, frankly, amazed that I found a pristine copy of this topical hardcover book at the *dollar store*, as it's only been out 3 years, and its theme and subjects are timeless. It appears to still be in print, but the new/used vendors over on Amazon are offering "very good" copies for as little as 1¢ (plus shipping). If you are sick and tired of the "treason media" and their zombie leftists drones, this will be a ray of sunshine in your life ... I highly recommend it!

Notes:

1. http://btripp-books.livejournal.com/68986.html

2-3. http://amzn.to/27p7pvt

Tuesday, March 17, 2009[1]

Not what I expected ...

As I've no doubt noted in this space in the past, I'm a good bit *obsessive* and will pretty much push through with any project (or book) that I've started. This is why it is so notable that I came very close to just *not finishing* The Mars Mystery: The Secret Connection Between Earth and the Red Planet[2].

Over the years, I've read of number of Graham Hancock's books, and have enjoyed his style, respected his research, and appreciated that he was far more *reserved* than many writing in the "ancient civilizations in contact with extraterrestrials" genre.

One of the "interesting factoids" that has come up in many books in the arena is that the Sphinx, a much older monument than the pyramids, is oriented so that it would have been looking at sunrise in the "age of Leo", some 10-12,000 years ago. I had assumed that the Sphinx/Pyramids stuff was going to dove-tail in with a perhaps more measured look at the "anomalies" of the Cydonia region on Mars than is usually found in the works of Hoagland et al. While this *is* an element of the book, it takes up perhaps only a quarter of the text, with the rest of it being astro-physical conjecture of a most unsettling sort.

Much of the first half of the book looks at Mars and asks *how* it got to be the battered dead planet that we see today. Half of Mars appears to have had its crust *blasted off*, and there are craters on its surface that are far in excess of the blast that caused the great Cretaceous-Tertiary extinction event on Earth. In a manner like the Shoemaker-Levy comet impacts seen on Jupiter in 1994, Hancock proposes that a large comet had a near head-on collision with Mars, and split into multiple chunks of various sizes, the largest literally *peeling* the crust off of half the planet.

Prior to this impact, Mars was a warmer, wet world, with oceans, rivers, and possibly even a breathable atmosphere. Very much like Earth.

Most of the book is Hancock's research on comets and asteroids. And how vulnerable Earth is to these. I hate to go into details that are still disturbing to me, but the second half of this book is SO steeped with a sense of *DOOM* that it can't help to depress the reader. The "Taurid stream" (which produces meteor showers twice a year) appears to be the "debris trail" of a monster comet whose only *visible* remnant is the comet Encke, but which is *filled* with massive "dark objects" (some of these reflect less than 4% of the light that hits them) which we wouldn't be able to see until *hours* before collision!

Hancock obviously spent a great deal of time cross-referencing dates from astronomical programs with geological and historical records, and comes up with some grim predictions. Not only does he suggest that the last ice age was ended by a massive impact, but that over the past 1500 years we've been in a rare quiet period, and may be *soon* entering into a phase where the Earth will be hit with Tunguska-or-bigger objects as many as *100 times a year.*

Again, one of the things I've always liked about Hancock's books is the intensive research that he puts into them, and in this case, it's very dark. Needless to say, he's STRONGLY advocating an international "near-Earth object" search and on-going watch, but it's depressing to see how little money is being spent on this currently.

One of the "wow" things in here is his suggestion that what happened to Mars did not happen in the vastly deep past ... in fact, he suggests that the comet/asteroid bombardment that killed Mars was the same one that ended the last ice age on Earth, as recently as 17,000 years ago. And that the Sphinx (and other monuments of anomalous vintage) are markers set to draw our attention to this event.

Again, The Mars Mystery[3] is NOT a "fun read". It has its moments of fascination, and is well done, but is *horribly depressing*. If you want to be scared shitless about the future of the planet, well here's a book for you. If you want to stay blissfully unaware of the dire threat we live under (literally, we could be bashed by a planet-ending object *any day* and have only *hours* of warning), you might want to skip this. If you feel up to it, Amazon has the paperback at 32% off, and their new/used vendors have copies of the hardcover "like new" for as little as $2.50 (plus shipping), plus it does appear to still be in print so your local bookstore will likely be able to hook you up with all the doom you can handle. Seriously, it's *that* unsettling.

Notes:

1. http://btripp-books.livejournal.com/69264.html
2-3. http://amzn.to/1WyET7t

Wednesday, March 18, 2009[1]
More than I really needed to know ...

Well, after that last book, I really needed some "mental floss" to get me back on an even keel, and if there's one thing that "Dover Thrift Editions" do as well as getting a book order up to that free-shipping promised land, it's providing a brief dip into a subject.

The subject at hand over the past couple of days has been Persian Poetry, specifically Hafiz. Now, most of the listings of <u>The Garden of Heaven: Poems of Hafiz</u>[2] list "Hafiz" as the author, but I'm afraid that this is a bit misleading, as Gertrude Bell is much more the author of this book, not only did she (admirably) translate the poems, but she wrote a rather in-depth (if "dated") 30-page Introduction to them, as well as 25 pages of detailed notes on the 40 pages of actual poems. Personally, I was in this for the *poems*, so was somewhat put off (OK, "nodded off" on the train) with the excess of exposition wrapped around them.

As with most of these Dover books, this is a re-print of an old release, in this case a volume originally published over a century ago, in 1897! As such, I'm able to cut the author (who appears to have been quite an adventurer and scholar) some slack on what could be seen from a modern perspective as a rather stiff view of Sufism.

Frankly, by the time I'd gotten through the introduction, I was rather apprehensive of how the poems would be presented, as Gertrude Bell was certainly living up to certain clichés of a "Victorian", but I was rather pleased with how the poems flowed. I always have certain doubts about translations of poetry that attempt to maintain a rhyme scheme, as even composing in one's native language a poet frequently has to do violence to the meaning in order to fit the rhyme, so I would guess that this is *not* the best translation if one is looking for "subtle Sufi truths", but as poetry, it's quite nicely rendered.

> *My heart, sad hermit, stains the cloister floor*
> *With drops of blood, the sweat of anguish dire;*
> *Ah, wash me clean, and o'er my body pour*
> *Love's generous wine! the worshipers of fire*
> *Have bowed them down and magnified my name,*
> *For in my heart there burns a living flame,*
> *Transpiercing Death's impenetrable door.*

If nothing else, Hafiz seems to have been remarkable in the way that he was able to keep afloat amidst the courts of a whole string of conquerors of his native Shiraz ... in fact, it would appear that for most of his life he was in demand, with various regional royalties almost "bidding" for his attendance.

Anyway, <u>The Garden of Heaven</u>[3] is quite an interesting little book, providing a two-tiered window, one into Victorian scholarship, and the other into 14th century Persian politics and poetry. This is still in print, at the princely cover price of $2.00 ... which makes it one of those "in reserve" titles to add in on a twenty-three-something book order!

Notes:

1. http://btripp-books.livejournal.com/69418.html

2-3. http://amzn.to/1Ytrn1W

Sunday, March 22, 2009[1]
Important, but not essential ...

If anybody has been "following along" and matching my reading over on LibraryThing[2] with my reviews here (yeah, there might be some out there without better hobbies!), you'd notice that I'm a dozen or so books behind on writing reviews, with a big clutch of them dating back to last October/November. Well, this book was somewhat to blame.

I'd brought Ron Paul's A Foreign Policy of Freedom: Peace, Commerce, and Honest Friendship[3] along with me on the trip I made to Florence, Italy last fall, figuring that it would be easy enough to knock down over two trans-Atlantic flights. Unfortunately, I had not counted on how slow a read this could be, and it ended up taking a the whole trip and then some to plow through.

Now, as regular readers of my main blog know, I'm a Ron Paul fan (albeit not a "rabid follower") and looked forward to reading this. What I hadn't figured in that this is, minus a paragraph here and there of introductory material, simply a collection of speeches that Rep. Paul has made from the floor of the House of Representatives. Yes, even the *concept* is deadening. Sam Kinnison would have been muted playing that hall. These range over a 30-year period, from a 1976 commentary on the death of Mao Tse Tung, to a 2006 note about dialog with Iran. While the specifics of Ron Paul's "concerns" have shifted in tone and focus over the decades, they still range within personal freedoms at home, and the very likely ill-advised attempts of turning our Republic into a global Empire.

As a "conservative Libertarian", the biggest shocker in here is the extent of our global military commitment. According to Paul, we have *over 700 bases in 130 countries* around the world. Can you *name* 130 countries?

While I don't necessarily agree with his stance that *none* of that military presence is needed, the financial burden of it is horrendous, and we have, essentially, made it possible for Western Europe to become the soft socialist morass it is by funding the bulk of their defense for the past 50 years. I'm certainly with him on the idiocy of domestic programs that use the weight of the government to steal from the productive citizens to coddle (read: buy the votes of) the unproductive, leading ourselves down that same disastrous socialist path.

Of course, given the nightmare scenario of leftist programs sinking the financial markets just in time to put a Communist in the office of the Presidency, many of the "niceties" that Paul addresses here seem to be drowned out by the tsunami of leftist insanity that is coming from Washington these days.

Frankly, in the current crisis, I would find it hard (unless one really wanted to see the *consistency* of Ron Paul's message) to recommend A Foreign

Policy of Freedom[4], being, long, dense, and (of nature) rambling. Better to go get a copy of Paul's The Revolution: A Manifesto[5], as *that's* what we need at the moment! Anyway, were you wanting to check this out, it is in print, and available at a discount from Amazon that as good as the cheapest used copies when combined with shipping.

Hopefully getting this out of my "to review" pile will break the logjam there!

Notes:

1. http://btripp-books.livejournal.com/69815.html
2. http://btripp-books.com/
3-4. http://amzn.to/27p5yXC
5. http://btripp-books.livejournal.com/62818.html

Saturday, March 28, 2009[1]

Had we only known ...

Sometimes it's useful to look back to where we were ... I have a stack of things here to review which were the view ahead from various GOP writers, all of whom sadly missed the coming storm that slammed into the U.S.A. and is destroying it even as I write this.

Amanda B. Carpenter's The Vast Right-Wing Conspiracy's Dossier on Hillary Clinton[2] isn't necessarily one of those, but is a sobering reminder of how *BAD* things are, and are likely to be for at least the next four years. I've read a lot about the Clintons, and *know* how bad Hillary is, but it was only a few months back that she was looking as an appealing alternative to the "stealth Communist" candidate and the RINO[3] in the last election. This book serves to remind me of how little she *actually* differs from the abomination in the White House.

The author, a reporter for *Human Events*, takes a slightly different approach from other warning tomes on Mrs. Clinton, first of all, claiming the "vast right-wing conspiracy" tag and wearing it with ironic pride, and the spinning off that ownership to thicken the irony with a graphic style in the book that highlights the "dossier" angle. Carpenter is less caustic than Ann Coulter, but does one thing that Ann has not (usually leaving her readers to follow up the extensive footnotes themselves), and this is reproducing vast amounts of documentation in the book.

This, frankly, leads to this being a rather fast read ... as the first half is the "reports" and the second half is the "exhibits" (or "evidence"), with the latter half being page after page of campaign finance reports, personal letters to people that Hillary claims to "not know", and sign-offs on illegal operations that either the First Lady or the Senator from New York flatly denies having ever heard of. While it doesn't make gripping reading, it's pretty damning to Mrs. Clinton.

The book is in ten "files", covering illegal campaign financing, her socialist plans in various areas, the *obscene* amount of "pork" she's channeled to New York to buy off voting blocs there, how the vile MSM has been an enabling lapdog for her both at the White House and in the Senate, and her constant flip-flops on subjects like Immigration, the War on Terror, and Gay Marriage, where she plays both to her hard-left core constituency and to "moderate" voters, counting on the media not to point out the totally different messages and promises being made depending on her audience.

Another useful part of this book is the reproduction of speeches and exchanges from the Congressional Record, transcripts from radio and TV appearances, and the like. Hillary can try to be an enigma to those not paying attention, but without her Media accomplices, she'd be seen as the conniving monomaniac she is to all but her "praetorian guard".

What is *less* useful here are the sections of "strategizing" on how to oppose the Presidential Campaign of Mrs. Clinton, with facts, figures, and names to bring up. Although only written in 2006, this is sadly dated, the country already having passed by the socialist frying pan to fall into the neo-Stalinist fire.

Oddly enough, The Vast Right-Wing Conspiracy's Dossier on Hillary Clinton[4] is still in print, but I got this copy at the dollar store, and the Amazon new/used vendors have copies from 1¢ for "like new" and 25¢ for "new". I'd recommend this for those who need to re-frame the context of just what madness we are being subjected to right now, and even to Hillary fans who still don't appreciate what a monster it is that they love so dearly.

Notes:

1. http://btripp-books.livejournal.com/70103.html
2. http://amzn.to/27p4XoE
3. http://en.wikipedia.org/wiki/Republican_In_Name_Only
4. http://amzn.to/27p4XoE

Monday, March 30, 2009[1]
Not quite what I was expecting ...

I got this book via the "Early Reviewers" program over at LibraryThing.com ... I suspect I would have gotten it anyway, as the good folks over at Hampton Roads publishing (http://hrpub.com) have been sending me out copies of their recent Buddhist books for review, but it's always fun to "win" one in the E.R. program (which regularly has 5-20 requests made for every available copy).

I would have, frankly, been surprised to have *not* gotten ten The Dalai Lama's Little Book of Inner Peace: The Essential Life and Teachings[2], having read extensively in the area of Tibetan Buddhism, and having taken numerous initiations from His Holiness over the years (The Kalachakra in Madison, L.A., and New York, and the Avalokitesvara in Madison and L.A.), reflected heavily in my library. Needless to say, I was pleased to have this come my way and that the "almighty Algorithm" (the way LT matches books with reviewers) worked again!

I was, however, expecting something more along the lines of the title, a book of, perhaps, meditations for "inner peace", etc., when it really is more like the *sub-title* "The Essential Life and Teachings". Interestingly, this book has been kicking around in other forms for a while, first being published in French in 1996, and then in English (under the title *The Spirit of Peace*) in 2002. Here the material has been reformatted to a "little book" (4.5x5.5"), which is deceivingly thick.

In my opinion, this book is a *very good* introduction to the Dalai Lama for those who don't know much about him. This is divided into six sections, beginning with a biographical section, with some explanation about the concepts of reincarnating Lamas, then moves into the situation with the Chinese takeover of Tibet, and the Dalai Lama's life in exile. Very little of these first two sections has much to do with "inner peace", except in relation to how His Holiness managed to keep his own equanimity in the face of his people being butchered by the Communists.

The rest of the book steps progressively into more esoteric areas, with "The World Today", "Faith, Science, and Religion", "The Inner Journey", and "Life, Death, and Rebirth". Again, this is not specifically about "inner peace" as it is brief, yet very clear, explanations of how Vajrayana approaches various aspects of one's existence. Here are a couple of excerpts:

> It is my profound belief that together we need to find a new form of spirituality. It should be developed in parallel with the religions, so that all those of goodwill can follow it, whether they are religious or not. One new concept, for example, is that of lay spirituality. We should promote this ideal with the help of the scientific community. It could help us establish what we are all looking for - secular eth-

ics. I believe in this deeply, with the view it will lead to a better world.

That's pretty amazing advocacy coming from the head of a 1,000-year theocracy! Throughout this book, He looks "outside the box" (or what one might expect his "box" to be) and seeks to find middle ground on various levels (one thing that may surprise many is that he has meat with his daily meals, partly on the recommendation of his doctors, partly in that it is very hard to maintain a wholly vegetarian diet in Tibet, so the traditional meals have had meat included). Here's another, on a bit more metaphysical topic:

> *Emptiness corresponds to the idea of zero, to the total absence of intrinsic existence. A zero, in itself is nothing, yet without zero counting is impossible. Therefore zero is something and nothing at the same time. The same goes for emptiness. Emptiness is empty, and at the same time it is the basis of everything.*

The Dalai Lama's Little Book of Inner Peace: The Essential Life and Teachings[3] is a new release, so should be available at your local book vendor (at its *very* low cover price), while both Amazon and the publisher have it discounted for less than ten bucks. For long-time followers of the Dalai Lama, there are only subtle surprises here, but for somebody wanting to find out what "the whole Tibetan thing" is about, this is a very useful, and accessible, introduction.

Notes:

1. http://btripp-books.livejournal.com/70291.html
2-3. http://amzn.to/1XcriBh

Saturday, April 11, 2009[1]

Well, that was interesting ...

Every once in a while I totally "whiff" on a book ... plowing into a text thinking that I'm reading something about "X" when I'm actually reading a book about "Y", and this was one of those cases. I'd found Jean-François Revel's Without Marx or Jesus: The New American Revolution Has Begun[2] referenced in something else that I was reading, and was (at the time) very pleased to discover that I was able to obtain a copy (via Amazon's new/used vendors), as it appears to have been out of print for quite a while.

Now, as regular readers of this space have probably figured out about me, I have very little patience for either Marxism/Socialism or the "major religions", so when I'd gotten wind of a book that was purportedly talking about "a new American revolution" that was "without Marx or Jesus", I was thrilled, as I was hoping to be delving into a treatise about how we were going to be building that non-Leftist Secular society, based on reason, "common sense", and meritocracy.

Well, that ain't this book. OK, so maybe this goes halfway there, with the "without Marx" part covered, but this is by no means the book that I had hoped that it was going to be. The author was a French political philosopher who, in the latter third of his life, decided to become something of a provocateur, writing a string of books that served to highlight the failings of various social situations and institutions. This is one of those books, and is focused less on America than it is pointing out the deficiencies of French, and European, cultural expectations.

One thing to bear in mind with this book is that it was written in *1970*. Revel had just come over to the U.S. for an extended stay, and had been caught up in the social changes boiling up in the late 60's. This particular slice of time in America probably gave him the wrong impression on how things were vectoring here, and led him to the central focus of this book, that "the revolution" was going to come out of the U.S.A. and not from Europe or the third world. Of course, part of this prediction was based on our "mass media" in a time when many European nations were barely experimenting with TV, having only a few hours of programming on 2-3 channels each day, so in many ways this book is a "time capsule" into a culture scarcely recognizable today.

Needless to say, I was disappointed that the "religion question" was barely touched on ... he briefly notes "Jesus Freaks" and eastern influences, compares the wide *variety* of churches in the U.S. to the tradition of Papist ecclesiastical control in Europe, but he never gets into the vast sea of blind belief that is middle America.

Again, this book was written for a *French* audience, addressing their preconceptions. He takes apart Russia, China, the Third World, and most of Socialist Europe as being *unable* to support the sort of revolution he was promoting (which was a move towards a "New World Order" with a planetary government, oddly similar to the goals of the similarly ex-resistance

"Sion" folks detailed in another book³ that I recently reviewed). Much of the book is spent in critiquing the rampant anti-Americanism of the French, and showing how remarkably misguided it was/is (obviously, from the current state of the Democratic Party, the sort of mindless anti-Americanism has not only survived but spread *to America*).

One thing I found very odd here was that the publishers had noted Trotsky-ite Mary McCarthy write an Afterword to the book, which seems rather contrary to much of the aims of the author, which in turn is pointed out by Revel in an "author's note" closing the book, where he refutes much of what's in the Afterword ... how odd for a writer to have to have this sort of a dust-up within the pages of their own book!

Anyway, Without Marx or Jesus⁴ is not the book that I was anticipating, and, while interesting, is so largely in a "sociological" sense of looking through it as a lens to a particular time. There are various versions of this book out there in the used channels, but unless you have a particular interest in any of the above, I don't see why you'd want to make the effort ... especially as the 1971 hardcover edition that I got in "very good" condition for $4.00 (plus shipping) is now showing up with a "good" copy at nearly $35.00!

Notes:

1. http://btripp-books.livejournal.com/70500.html
2. http://amzn.to/1XcimeW
3. http://btripp-books.livejournal.com/67093.html
4. http://amzn.to/1XcimeW

Sunday, April 12, 2009[1]

Disappointing ...

This was one of my "dollar store" acquisitions, so wasn't something that I specifically went looking for, but I guess I was hoping for more *attitude* in G. Gordon Liddy's Fight Back: Tackling Terrorism, Liddy Style[2]. Perhaps because this is a "team effort" (it's co-authored with his ex-seal son, an emergency medicine MD, and a defense department terrorism expert) it mutes what I was expecting from the "Liddy Style" ... as this reads a lot more like a government manual than his seminal book *Will*!

The book is in three sections, "Know Your Enemy", "Secure Yourself", and an "Emergency/Terrorism Response Handbook" (it's the former in the index, the latter in the page headings). While there are fascinating bits of data in each of these sections (such as an analysis of various bio weapons in the third part), the most interesting elements are in the beginning where (I'm assuming) G.G.L. is providing his "take" on the various threats out there.

The problem I had with the book is that there isn't very much in here to "help" a standard family with a standard budget. I don't think in our apartment that I'd be able to build in a "safe room" (especially with the dimensions suggested), and unless one's a Mormon, it would involve a *substantial* re-working of priorities to simply *stock* the supplies recommended. Much of the "take-away" here is that the main target of this are corporations and their CEO's, as substantial parts of the book are dealing with how to set up the exteriors of office and factory buildings and how to avoid getting kidnapped (including such useful information as the optimal angle and speed to take a curb in order to drive off on the sidewalk).

Again, I suppose that I had hoped to have been exposed to more of the acerbic Liddy wit here, but that is in very short supply, and is largely limited to a re-print of a "fictionalized" White House memo, originally published in Omni magazine, detailing a disastrous series of attacks on the US.

Speaking of re-prints, I was somewhat surprised at how much the book uses out-takes from assorted state and federal government publications. Given the team assembled to work on this book, one would think they'd have been able to come up with more focused material than quoting the Rhode Island Department of Health.

If one's not in a position to free up a large amount of money for "preparedness", I'm afraid that Fight Back[3] is a pretty grim read, as it's basically outlining "how you're screwed" rather than how one might "fight back" or "tackle terrorism". As I noted, this "like new" (it has one small black marker dot on one edge) hardcover came from the dollar store, even though it's still "in print" (Amazon is offering it at a 42% discount). The new/used guys have this for as low as a penny (plus shipping, of course), so if you're interested in reading it, and can't run across it for $1, that is likely your best bet for getting this.

Notes:
1. http://btripp-books.livejournal.com/70801.html
2-3. http://amzn.to/1XchpDB

Sunday, April 12, 2009[1]

Conspiracies etc.

Let me preface this by saying that I firmly believe that there are whole areas of "physics" that have only been glancingly dealt with by the scientific mainstream. Unfortunately, because there is no visible "big science" work being done in these areas, the news that comes out about what work *is* being done is almost by definition from "the fringe" ... but this material is fascinating and tends to provide "answers" about various things that are very enticing. I've read a lot of this in various places on the web, usually starting with Richard C. Hoagland's archives[2].

In following links around I had frequently run into citations from Joseph P. Farrell's books, and when I encountered his Secrets of the Unified Field: The Philadelphia Experiment, The Nazi Bell, and the Discarded Theory[3], I was hoping that it was going to be looking at the *science* behind the effects that he refers to as "torsion" and Hoagland labels "hyperdimensional".

Unfortunately, with the exception of looking at some of the developments of Einstein's thought (the "Discarded Theory" of the sub-title was the Unified Field Theory), this book is very little about the science and was all about the "conspiracies", especially those that various researchers have "found" around "The Philadelphia Experiment". I wonder why the author didn't just write a book on that, as this book only runs about 1/8th of its length looking at the work of Einstein and related theorists at the start, then goes on and on about the Philadelphia Experiment, and finally gives a brief "conspiracy" over-view of the "Nazi Bell" project, a subject the author has written extensively on elsewhere, but barely gives enough info on here to provide the reader a clue to what it was or was supposed to do, let alone how it was supposed to do it!

Now, I don't want to specifically say that I wasn't particularly interested in the Philadelphia Experiment, but it's one of those things that has rumors WAY out of control around it, and is one of those military projects that one is not likely to ever get a straight answer on one way or the other. I *was*, however, very interested in the possibility of delving into the *science* behind these various "secret projects". Regrettably, this was not much in evidence here, making the whole story another web of suggestive paper trails and fantastic stories of accidentally time-traveling bystanders.

Obviously, if the more extreme effects reported about the "Philadelphia Experiment" and the "Nazi Bell" could be proven true, the science made repeatable, and the whole process harnessed to some functional goal, this would be reality-changing, but sixty years later there's no sign of any technology that would seem to be rooted in these systems, which makes me think that it's all chasing rumors and creating conspiracies to explain why there's no straight answers.

Of course, if one approached this sort of material looking for an emotional charge from the "woo woo" conspiracy stuff, this book would be right up your alley ... but if you're looking for a cogent walk-through of the science related to these subjects, like I was, you're likely to be sorely disappointed.

What's almost as irritating is that I actually paid "retail" (well, Amazon's 32% -off price) for this, and I can't give you an alternative (the cheapest used copy there is almost the same price). Again, if you're looking for "oooh, big military/government conspiracy!" twaddle, you'll love this, otherwise save your money.

Notes:

1. http://btripp-books.livejournal.com/71037.html
2. http://www.enterprisemission.com/NewsArchive.html
3. http://amzn.to/1WyuyIt

Saturday, April 18, 2009[1]

Verrrrrry eeenteresting ... but Dated!

I wonder why it is that it took me pretty much till my late 40's and into my 50's to be interested in reading *business* books. Not that this is major focus of my reading over-all, but I find myself every now and again buried in a book about business, and not being bored out of my mind!

Of course, I've not been running out to the *bookstore* to pay *retail* for these ... I believe this one came from that "fill a shopping bag for $5" sale a year or so back, or might have shown up at the dollar store. However, I've been interested in how *interesting* some of the few books I've picked up along these lines have been. Rolling it around in my mind, I think that five or six years when I *refused* to read any fiction may have shifted my tastes away from what I'd previously found engaging.

Anyway, for some reason, out of the vast stacks of to-be-read books sitting around here, Larry Kahaner's Competitive Intelligence: How to Gather Analyze and Use Information to Move Your Business to the Top[2] seemed the best bet for my "transit book" this week.

As regular readers of this space will be all too aware of, one of my on-going "challenges" in the recent necessity of my acquiring most of my books from used sources is that frequently the books I'm consuming are a bit dated. This one isn't particularly *old*, having come out in 1996, but for a book about amassing *information*, that's *ancient* (heck, that was the same year that I put up my first website, for my old publishing house, Eschaton Books). The author spends a non-insignificant number of pages early on in this "letting the reader know" about this amazing new thing that lets you get information through the computer ... you might have heard of it, the World Wide Web.

Needless to say, 13 years up that technology curve, much of what he talks about in terms of commercial and governmental databases seems rather quaint (not that some of the corporate by-subscription resources have lost their importance for serious research) in relation to what is available to any 8-year-old today ... so many of the *activity details* of the book need to be taken with a grain or two of salt.

I'm not sure *where* exactly, the Competitive Intelligence field is these days ... I've been out of the "big corporation" game for a long time, so I've not been in situations where I'd notice a *department*, but either they've become so common that they go unmentioned, or that the "intelligence" function has been so broadly distributed that it no longer exists as a free-standing group reporting to the CEO.

Perhaps the most interesting, and possibly least stale, part of this book is his analysis of how various other nations have these sorts of functions organized. Many, notably Japan and France, have companies working hand-in-hand with the government, where Corp. A can actually *hire* the equivalent of their CIA to go get a particular piece of information ... others, like many old Soviet-bloc 3rd world countries, use their training as Soviet stand-ins to freelance intel to the highest bidder. Of course, writing in the immediate wake of the collapse of the Soviet Union, much of this was in flux ... and how could he know as he was writing this that the Clintons were actively colluding with the PRC to sell military tech for *campaign contributions*?

There are lots of fascinating snippets in here about places where bribery is so common (say, you're in line at the DMV, and can "tip" somebody to save an hour of waiting) that it's all a grey area when it comes to government resources, to the tales of the Japanese who'd send in 20 or so families into an Arabic-speaking nation for a 10-year posting just to get "the feel" of the culture, etc.

While most of his stories are of *others* stripping the USA bare, he does have some refreshing anecdotes of American companies very successfully using Competitive Intelligence in situations where they took it seriously, and were not hindered by the Government.

Given the above caveats, it's not surprising that Competitive Intelligence[3] is no longer in print, however, it *is* available via the after-market, with Amazon's guys having "very good" copies for as little as 18¢ and "new" copies from $4.44 (plus shipping, of course, in both cases), should this sound like something you want to add to your mental file (and library).

Notes:

1. http://btripp-books.livejournal.com/71280.html
2-3. http://amzn.to/1WzEBwr

Saturday, April 18, 2009[1]

Finally - a FABULOUS book!

Are you, the regular readers of this space, as tired of reading "disappointed" reviews as I am of writing them? I realize that out of the last couple of dozen books I've reviewed I've barely managed to get past a grunt as far as enthusiasm goes, which is why I'm doubly excited to be writing about Joan Parisi Wilcox's Masters of the Living Energy: The Mystical World of the Q'ero of Peru[2], which is a really fabulous book!

Now, I have to admit, I was *very* hesitant when I first picked this up, I've been "burned" so many times on books on Peruvian Shamanism (even by authors with whom I'm acquainted), finding woo-woo and wishful thinking in place of actual information and background. Admittedly, I'm a harsh critic, having studied "Incan" shamanic traditions for well over a decade back in the 80's and 90's, and having worked in Peru with Quechuan teachers, and in the US with visiting Q'ero (and "carrying lineages" from both traditions, along with a "mesa"). Needless to say, I was *delighted* to find the tone and approach of this book being very level-headed, yet "informed".

Frankly, I'm surprised that I hadn't encountered this book in its previous manifestation, having been published by Element as *Keepers of the Ancient Knowledge* in 1999, preceding this Inner Traditions "revised edition" paperback by five years.

It appears from the into section that Ms. Wilcox initially went to Peru on one of Alberto Villoldo's[3] trips (as I had, perhaps a decade previously), due to a passing mention of him, and some "familiar" patterns of places/activities. She evidently became more connected with Peruvian teachers such as Américo Yábar and Juan Nuñez del Prado, and forged her own path through them towards interacting with the Q'ero.

The book is divided into four fairly logical sections ... *The Kawsay Pacha: The World of Living Energy*, where she discusses the over-all world-view of the Q'ero ... *Walking the Sacred Path: Interviews with the Q'ero*, which allows her to get into more detail of the Q'ero, without necessarily having to *explain* things ... *Our Heart's Fire: The Mesa and Healing*, this discusses more of the "systems" involved in the Q'ero's practices, and the nature of their training ... and *The Flight of the Condor: Putting Andean Practices to Work in Your Life* in which she presents several very useful exercises and lets in a little bit of the "mystical" aspect of the Q'ero teachings.

As I've noted, this is all very well done, but there are some things that could have been improved. First of all, there is a *wonderful* 9-page "Glossary of Andean Mystical Terms" in the back of the book which helps to define (and pronounce: would *you* have guessed that *Kawsay* was said COW-sigh?) various Quechuan/Q'ero words used in the book, but this is not comprehensive, there are many instances where a word is introduced in the text (and even italicized to hint that it's defined) but never adequately addressed. Her editors should be rapped across the knuckles with a wooden ruler for not adding those to the Glossary, and insisting that Ms. Wilcox come up with at least an approximate pronunciation and basic definition! The other irritating thing here is that she spends a not insignificant amount of verbiage explaining how the interviews with the Q'ero were limited in time and they didn't get to stuff she wanted to ask, etc. Now, I, obviously, don't have a clue about how "connected" she is to the various westernized teachers/shamen she works with, but it seems to me that if she had to limit the actual interview process, she could have made up for it with an on-going mail exchange with the likes of Americo, Juan, or Fredy "Puma" Quispe Singona (who even came to stay with her in the States), folks who have in-depth personal ties to the Q'ero who should have been able to fill in some of the gaps.

These quibbles aside, Masters of the Living Energy[4] is a really excellent book, and one I'm happy that I actually paid (Amazon's discounted) retail for! In fact, if you're going to get this, that's likely your best bet, as the used vendors only have it for a buck or so off of Amazon's price, so double it up with another book and you'll be ahead with the free shipping.

Again, if you have *any* interest in the "Mystical Q'ero" (who had been thought of only as "legends" before their re-appearance in the late-50's!), this is probably the most *legitimate* over-view that's out there ... highly recommended!

Notes:

1. http://btripp-books.livejournal.com/71456.html
2. http://amzn.to/1rNdUrz
3. http://thefourwinds.com/
4. http://amzn.to/1rNdUrz

Sunday, April 19, 2009[1]

Not his best ...

Over the years, I've read quite a number of Paul Davies' books, which are usually entertaining while still being informative on their subject. This one, Are We Alone?: Philosophical Implications Of The Discovery Of Extraterrestrial Life[2], just seemed to "miss me".

Perhaps it was the format ... this is a collection of six essays (plus some additional material) presented as *lectures* at the University of Milan over *two days* back in 2003, each running somewhere around 20 pages. I assume that, being a college professor, Davies would not be daunted at presenting six lectures over two days (as opposed to most business speakers), but the format does *not* lend itself to particular depth on any topic. Also, as per the sub-title, everything he's approaching here has an over-laid "philosophical" spin, so not only does he have to present a "getting up to speed" scan of a topic, put it out within the context of "Are We Alone?", but then step into philosophizing over the various implications.

The topics here are: "A Brief History of SETI", "Extraterrestrial Microbes", "Alien Message", "The Nature of Consciousness", and "Alien Contact and Religious Experience", along with appendixes on "Project Phoenix" and "The Argument for Duplicate Beings" (which obsessive readers of this space may recall was a notable point in a book[3] reviewed a few months back).

Frankly, I was made somewhat uncomfortable several times in this book where Davies seems to be making a point to push into "philosophies" amenable to his Papist hosts by taking somewhat uncalled-for shots at the likes of Richard Dawkins and Stephen Jay Gould (ala "The Neo-Darwinian Contingency Argument"). Fortunately, it eventually becomes clear that he is not so much arguing against antitheistic stances as he is arguing for the "crystal-like" tendency towards complexity, and, ultimately, consciousness.

Of course, one of the core arguments for the "we're alone" forces is that if there *were* other beings out there, and there were some that were more advanced than us, then how come we haven't (despite on-going efforts) *found* any? One model he charts out is that of "planet hopping" colonization, where creatures (or their more-or-less sentient machines) would spread out across all the occupiable planets in the Galaxy within a span as short (!) as a million years. In a Galaxy that's 15 *billion* years old, that's a blink of an eye, and should have happened repeatedly.

Anyway, while there *are* interesting bits like this in here, the book as a whole is a something of a meander ... trying to stay within a thematic concept, and an over-lying "spin", it skips in and out of various concepts, without really providing a substantial look at any. Not surprisingly, this hasn't managed to stay in print (unlike many of Davies' other titles), but is available in the used market. The Amazon guys have "acceptable" copies for as little as a penny, with "like new" copies starting around two bucks. This isn't a *bad* book, just nowhere near the author's better efforts.

Notes:

1. http://btripp-books.livejournal.com/71871.html
2. http://amzn.to/1TDEGZM
3. http://btripp-books.livejournal.com/64337.html

Tuesday, April 21, 2009[1]
Something interesting ...

Sometimes a used book tells a story, above and beyond the book itself. There's a group over on LibraryThing.com called "Found in a Book" and I posted[2] a thing over there about a post card that was in this book. It's amazing how that sort of thing can "personalize" a book that moved through somebody else's life before getting into your hands. I picked up this at the Newberry Library Book Fair last summer, which is a pretty good indication that the original owner had died, nearly 35 years after getting the holiday greetings that seem to have been serving as a bookmark.

Anasazi: Ancient People of the Rock[3] came out in January of 1974, and had the rather steep cover price of $18.50 (that's about $85.00 in today's dollars!), fairly high for a book under 200 pages. It is, however, quite a striking photo tour of the Anasazi and related groups' ruins in the southwest. Photographed by David Muench, and with quite informative text by Donald G. Pike (who was not above adding humorous twists such as *"The Basket Makers responded with fur blankets and mantles. The raw material was supplied, albeit reluctantly, by the ubiquitous rabbit ..."*).

Structurally, the book goes back and forth between a substantial essay on the culture and area (briefly illustrated with photos of pottery, petroglyphs, various woven bits, etc.), and a portfolio of pictures of the ruins. Sites covered include Mesa Verde, Kayenta, Sinagua, Salado, Chaco Canyon, among others, including at the end a brief bit on the still-occupied mesa of Acoma, which the authors place in a linear descent from the Anasazi.

When I picked this up, I was sort of expecting it to be *just* a "picture book", but it did take me several days of sitting down with it to actually get through the text portions, which are nicely balanced on breadth and focus, each essay being on a particular topic, but all hanging together as a coherent narrative. The pictures are, of course, *glorious*.

I've been fortunate to have been able to have visited many of the sites covered here, and it's made me want to dig our my photos to see how *I saw* the ruins when we were out there. It was amusing to me that I was recalling one site (the restored Grand Kiva at Aztec Monument) from Pike's descriptions, and suddenly be looking at a picture of it (my elder daughter was about 3 when we went there, and was riding on my shoulders most of the time, so I have fond memories from there).

Anyway, Anasazi: Ancient People of the Rock[4] is a goodie, and if you can find a copy of it (and have an interest in the Anasazi), you should definitely consider picking it up. The hardcover I have looks to start around $20, but copies of the paperback can be found for a couple of bucks. Well worth looking for!

Notes:
1. http://btripp-books.livejournal.com/72187.html
2. http://www.librarything.com/topic/62907
3-4. http://amzn.to/1TeWhHO

Thursday, May 21, 2009[1]

Back to reviewing?

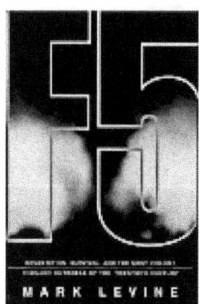

Yes, I have been slipping further behind in my book reviewing, I know, with 16 books in the stack to be reviewed. As those of you who have been reading my sparse postings in my blog know, my company is falling apart, although I'm still putting significant hours in working from home, I'm having to start looking for a job (in this lovely economy), and The Wife just got laid off. I'm doing 18 hour days, and not making up any ground ... sooooo, the book reviews keep not getting written. I'm in a state tonight where I just couldn't do another networking letter, nor start on a work project, so I'm hoping I can knock down a few titles before I pass out at the keyboard.

Anyway, this is a brand new book, having turned up just a couple of weeks back at the dollar store ... F5: Devastation, Survival, and the Most Violent Tornado Outbreak of the 20th Century[2] by Mark Levine is, as one might guess from the sub-title, a recounting of a devastating weather disaster that happened in northern Alabama in April, 1974. The book is a bit confusing, however, as it was written in 2007, about a storm that happened 33 years earlier, so one might think that the author had some connection to the events. However, the author was born in New York City, grew up in Canada, would have been about 9 years old at the time of the storm, and is primarily known for his poetry. What brought him to this subject? The only clue I can find is that this is "a Miramax book", and might have been penned as a companion book to a movie project.

The fact that Levine is not a "regular" nonfiction writer comes through in the back-and-forth telling of the tale, generally alternating chapters of reporting on what was happening in the US during April 1974, a bit of history on meteorological research (focusing on Dr. Tetsuya Fujita, whose last name graces the tornado intensity scale he developed, hence the "F5" of the title), and "personal stories" of various people caught up in the disaster that hit Limestone County, AL. Unfortunately, this does not "meld" very well, and is more like having had 3 separate books pulled apart and then collated (well, except for the Fujita parts, as he is pretty much "background" info until the very end) chronologically.

The most fascinating part of this, to me at least, was the description of how the weather ended up building up such a ferocious storm front (there were 148 twisters hitting in 24 hours over a dozen states in a broad band ranging from Chicago to Atlanta), which would have been the core of a very interesting book on meteorology, perhaps coupled with the historical background on the science (but at that point it would be a book about Dr. Fujita). However the "soul" of the book deals with the reconstructed stories of a few dozen people, in various family and professional groupings, and how the storm impacted their lives. The problem is, as these stories were told in isolated vignettes, it became hard as the book went on to really tell apart the people, and sort out their back stories. A lot of them died, many were mutilated, some are still alive today, but by the end of the book they all just sort of blend into "people affected by the storm".

Again, my guess is that this book was part of a movie project, and that (given that there is no mention of a movie in it) Miramax opted to just put out the book at some point. As a free-standing work, however, it's highly uneven and difficult to really "get into". This is not to say that it's not *interesting* in its various parts, just that the level of engagement is pretty low.

As noted above, I got this at the dollar store (with a sticker that indicated that it had been through Target's inventory at some point), so it's likely available in the aftermarket. Oddly (as if sometimes the case with what I find at the dollar store), Amazon seems to have it at their standard discount from cover, and even the new/used guys are asking nearly $3 for a "new" copy (plus shipping, of course). It's not a bad book, and if you're interested in violent weather, a bit of science history, or following folks around in the midst of a disaster, this could be something you'd want to pick up.

Notes:

1. http://btripp-books.livejournal.com/72403.html
2. http://amzn.to/224jDWl

Thursday, May 21, 2009[1]

Another of these ...

OK, maybe it's the *color scheme*, but every time I pick up a "for Dummies" book I get that nasty guilt thing that all English Majors get when coming in contact with a Cliffs Notes volume! I generally reserve these for situations where I've *learned something* sometime in the past, and have forgotten most of it (be the subject wine or Visual Basic) via disuse, yet know that I *knew* it and just need to have those synapses cleaned up and firing again.

Manny Hernandez's Ning for Dummies[2] is rather a different situation in that it's pretty much *the only reference* for the Ning social-networking platform (on which I'm developing various sites for friends/clients), and I *needed* this as a short-cut to get around some of the steeper learning curves involved!

Of course, there are challenges to reviewing a "how-to" book that take me out of my standard non-fiction "comfort zone", and especially in that I told the author (via Twitter communications) that I would be reviewing his book ... so I'm likely to be trying to stay more on-topic here than one might expect if this was not the case.

Now, as noted, I have been involved in working with Ning sites for the past 6-9 months, being part of a team that produced a half a dozen projects based on the platform, so I probably have much more familiarity with it than most people coming to the book. However, I was not the "tech lead" on any but the ones that I'm personally working on, so the "crunchier" bits were always lurking just behind the curtain. That said, my initial impression of Ning for Dummies[3] was that it was pretty much *three books*, one for total beginners, one for mid-level users, and one for folks (like me) who wanted or needed to "get under the hood". I didn't start sticking in slips of paper (for bookmarks) until Chapter 12, towards the end of part 3 (out of 6) so a bit over half the book was "stuff I knew" (albeit there were things laid out in a clearer manner than I'd ever encountered them), and a bit less than half of the book dealing with stuff that I'd either not figured out yet, or hadn't had to deal with (such as the parts of "marketing" the site within the Ning universe).

One substantial problem the book has can hardly be laid at the feet of the author, however, as this comes from the rapid pace of development that Ning has been going through. I follow several Ning feeds on Twitter, and there are new developments coming out *weekly*, so as new as this is, it's going to be very quickly outdated!

There are currently over *a million* Ning-based sites out there, ranging from the huge (half a million members on rapper 50¢'s site) to the tiny ... and with this book, I'm pretty sure that anybody with basic web-sense (and a smattering of HTML) could add another one in a couple of hours if they were so inclined. The first third of the book is *very* basic, and walks the reader step-by-step through what they need to do to start up a Ning-platform site.

The second third of the book pretty much bridges between the intro and expert levels, with a lot of very useful "now you do *this*" instructions that clarify a lot of things which are not particularly intuitive. Then, of course, there are the "under the hood" parts, as well as bits about getting people to join up (I was referring to a section in here just this afternoon to get over a problem that had come up on one site).

Since this is brand new, you're not likely to get any price break on it (aside from Amazon's 34% discount), but if you're wanting to do a Ning site, and don't have patience to try to dig through the less-than-stellar instructions that Ning has to offer, Ning for Dummies[4] will help!

Notes:
1. http://btripp-books.livejournal.com/72566.html
2-4. http://amzn.to/1Nt41Jk

Friday, May 22, 2009[1]
This usually doesn't happen ...

I think this is the last of the books that I got at that $5/ bag sale at AfterWords books a year or so back (although I haven't *reviewed* them all, I'm pretty sure I've *read* them all at this point). This was the "prize" of that, a big beautiful book, in very good condition, and I was very pleased with myself scoring it for as little as it worked out I paid for it.

You can imagine my embarrassment, when I logged Charles A Goodrum's Treasures of the Library of Congress[2] into my LibraryThing[3] catalog, that I found that I already had a copy in my library! Now, I have a lot of big "coffee table" books that I bought "back in the day" when I was a Public Relations exec pulling down six figures, and this must have been one of the books I added back then, but I had NO recall of it as I read through this ... suggesting to me that I probably had it sitting around more for "looks" than anything else at the time.

As it turns out, I was missing something, because this was quite the interesting read ... both from the standpoint of the history, mission, and changing priorities of the Library of Congress, and the details of the specific collections. The book must have been a daunting challenge to develop, as the LOC holdings are so vast ... some of the choices seem odd (for instance, tracing the development of the musical *Oklahoma!*) but are put in there to show how the various elements that are in the Library can work together for research, etc.

Generally speaking, however, the book is set up on "themes", many of them not books, it covers maps, and art, and photography, it looks at science, and "Orientalia", and historical documents, and musical instruments, and archival materials relating to Presidents, etc. At every turn there are superlatives, the most this, the most that, the most complete other thing, and the remarkable ways that many of these items found their way into the LOC.

Needless to say, as a former publisher, I was aware of one of the main ways the collection was built, as "back in the day" (I believe the requirement has been lifted, but I'm not sure) one had to submit two copies of everything one was getting copyright filed on to have the application processed. So, everything that was going to have an official US copyright registration ended up at least passing through their hands (a lot of ephemera, like, I suspect, my "chapbook" poetry collections got discarded).

This came out in 1980, and given the subject, *does* have a slightly dated feel, as computers were only just developing past room-sized leviathans at that point, and the cataloging of the collection was still very much a cards-in-a-drawer system when this was being written!

Treasures of the Library of Congress[4] does appear to be out of print, but I was *shocked* to find that it is available for very little (especially given the substantial weight and size of the book), with the Amazon new/used vendors having "very good" copies *under a buck* and "new" copies for as little as $3.25 (plus shipping, of course)! Given what it would cost to mail this, even at book rate, I'd think those guys (who have to agree to a flat-rate shipping fee) are selling it at a loss.

Anyway, this is a remarkable look at a remarkable institution, filled with amazing photos of amazing stuff, and held together by some very well-crafted prose. Especially given the prices that this can be had for, I'd highly recommend it as a great addition to anybody's library.

Notes:

1. http://btripp-books.livejournal.com/72731.html
2. http://amzn.to/1Nt3EyE
3. http://btripp-books.com/
4. http://amzn.to/1Nt3EyE

Friday, May 22, 2009[1]
So, dat's your story, comrade?

Ah, the mysterious joys of digging into my "to be read" cases of books ... this one could very well have been sitting around for over *a quarter century*, as it's a "book club edition" (that was likely a throw-in with another order) with a publication date of 1983!

The Russian Version of the Second World War: The History of the War As Taught to Soviet Schoolchildren[2], edited by Graham Lyons, is a window into (as one would gather from the subtitle) how the Soviets defined the war to their youth. The material in this book is taken from two standard Soviet text books, aimed at high school-aged students, one which focuses on the military history, and one that focuses on the political history. These materials were developed in 1956, following the death and official denouncement of Joseph Stalin. Prior to that, what few Soviet military histories there were, were "all about Stalin" and he only gets mentioned in passing a few times in these texts.

This was very much like reading an "alternative reality" book ... where the general outlines of events were familiar, but all the detail and framing had changed. There were multiple points that just seemed strange. The one that most stood out to me was the constant inclusion of political operatives in various military operations ... as though nothing could happen unless a Communist Party functionary was on hand and making sure that everybody was in a "revolutionary fervor" ... sort of like a union foreman on a job site or something! It was also odd seeing the term "Hitlerites" when referring to the Germans ... of course, when these texts were written, half of Germany was a Soviet puppet state, so I guess they didn't want to smear the German people with the Nazi acts, but also didn't want to use "Nazi" as that would besmirch Socialism!

The other notable aspect is the flip-flop of how we tend to view things ... the Allies are seen as collaborators with the Nazis in the case of Finland, the Soviet annexation of much of Poland is framed as just "neighbors moving through to fight the Germans". The book constantly harps on how "easy" the Allies had it, how the Germans hardly fought at all on the Western front, and how there was a Big Huge Conspiracy to have the Nazis and the Communists pretty much destroy each other (OK, so that's not so far-fetched). The Japanese (and Pacific theater) are scarcely mentioned unless in context of their being a threat on the far eastern edges of the Soviet empire, and the Allied campaigns around the Mediterranean are pretty much just dismissed. Now, admittedly, the Soviets did fend off the Germans, and broke the power of the "Nazi war machine", but the book plays it out like they did it unassisted, or even with one hand tied behind their back.

And, as one would expect, none of the Soviet atrocities are even alluded to ... while the "Hitlerites" were painted with that brush at every opportunity. Frankly, reading this was a little bit like watching *The Sopranos* ... it's a look inside a system where brutality, suppression, and the like are just part of the furnishings, and only *get* brought up when one of *your guys* gets whacked; a look into a world where totalitarian communist dictatorships are *needed* to be installed in every corner of the planet, and anything that goes against that is somehow criminal. Hmmm ... sounds like a faculty lounge at most universities!

Anyway, The Russian Version of the Second World War[3] is, understandably (after so many years) out of print, but "very good" copies can be had from the Amazon new/used vendors for under three bucks (plus shipping), and there are even some "like new" copies kicking around out there for a bit more. Again, this is sort of a trip down the rabbit-hole, so will appeal to a wider range of readers than one might think, if any of the above sounds like it's for you, it'll be a fascinating read!

Notes:

1. http://btripp-books.livejournal.com/72976.html

2-3. http://amzn.to/224gWEa

Friday, May 22, 2009[1]
A different angle on Gurdjieff ...

I've read a lot of Gurdjieff/Ouspensky/Bennett/etc. books over the years, and I'm frankly amazed at how many "angles" there are from which one can come at the Work. Admittedly, as the years roll on, there's less authenticity in the material (as it seems that none of their students ever got to the point of having something systematic, beyond the core books themselves, to pass on to the next generation), but it is interesting to see where it goes (like the "corporate enneagram" crap that *totally* has lost the concept of "outside shocks" *essential* to the model's functioning!).

This book, Views from the Real World: Early Talks Moscow, Essentuki, Tiflis, Berlin, London, Paris, New York, and Chicago as Recollected by His Pupils[2], attributed *to* Gurdjieff (but, obviously at one remove) is fascinating as it's the first step away from the his direct teachings (in that these were produced *by memory* by their transcribers, as Gurdjieff would not allow note-taking), but are also one of the clearest views *into* his teachings.

I really need to get over my hesitancy to mark up my books ... I had a half a dozen slips of paper stuck in this marking places that, as I was reading, seemed to hold particularly apt bits to quote in a review, however, out of context of the book, these are frequently hard to discover ... perhaps I need to move to sticky notes where I could "bracket" the section in question on the note! In this case, these appear to have been particularly lucid expositions of such things as Gurdjieff's concept of "octaves", of bodily postures (the area that his famous "stop" exercise was intended to highlight), the above-mentioned "shocks", the production of intentional non-subjective art, the various "centers" and "foods" of the being (and how the phrase *"I wish to remember myself"* triggers various of these in sequence), and subjects such as morality, suffering and consciousness, etc. I guess if you're interested, you'll have to get the book!

This is structured oddly, with sections based on the opening phrases of a talk, or just on their subject, with some being long (the whole of Section I is "Glimpses of Truth" which was in circulation early enough to have been mentioned in Ouspensky's *In Search of the Miraculous*) and some being just a few paragraphs. In all cases (as I recall) they are anonymous, leading me to wonder who *collected* them for publication, as these are from far-flung sources (as noted in the lengthy sub-title) and over a fairly wide span of years. After all, if Gurdjieff did not want his students taking notes, these would very likely have been "kept in secret" until after his death, or shared in very limited groups which were more interested in the literal exposition of the teachings than the Teacher's wishes about the teachings. It is also odd that, as far as I've been able to research it, this was published in 1973, while the materials in it range from 1917 to 1930, with Gurdjieff dying in 1949. Was this collected before his death, soon after his death, or much later?

Anyway, the material here is of specific interest as it's first-hand reports of Gurdjieff's teachings, even if those reports had to depend on the student's memory. Each is a moment in time with Gurdjieff, and most provide fascinating glimpses at nuances not necessarily present in the "canon" of what he wrote.

Views from the Real World[3] is still in print, so would be available at your local brick-and-mortar book vendor, although Amazon has it at just over ten bucks, which is a pretty good deal (the new/used copies start at $2.50, so with shipping that's almost there anyway). Some have suggested that this is a "good introduction" to Gurdjieff, but I disagree, as this is something that opens up parts of the teachings to students of Gurdjieff's written material, and it would be better to start with that (perhaps *Meetings with Remarkable Men*) and then pick this up after absorbing some of the materials that he intended to convey to a general audience. However, if you're interested, this should not hold you back from getting a copy of the book.

Notes:

1. http://btripp-books.livejournal.com/73444.html
2-3. http://amzn.to/1UYzULu

Saturday, May 23, 2009[1]

Duty ...

This book review is brought to you by the heavy hand of OCD ... I just *couldn't allow* myself to "take a pass" on doing a review because I had decided some years ago to write a review for *every book* I read. (Now I just need to work on the concept of *timely* reviewing, still having a dozen waiting-to-be-reviewed books going back as far as last November ... yeah, my impressions on *those* will be real *fresh*, not!)

One of things I've observed about myself that I have a hard time syncing with my self-image is that I *really* don't care for Philosophy. I love reading a wide range of non-fiction, and as anybody who's meandered through my LibraryThing[2] catalog can tell, I have a fairly eclectic taste in what I'll pick up, but every time I find myself in a "philosophy" book, I can't wait to get *done* with it, and then can't find much to say about it once I'm finished.

Anyway, as I've noted in this space previously, I've been trying to "plug some holes" in my basic education, finding that in a lot of cases I know *about* something but have not read the actual texts involved (hence the amount of Nietzsche I've plowed through in the past year or so). Sure, I could blither on about Socrates, Plato, and Aristotle, and hit most of the high points, but I probably only got through text-book excerpts back in high school and college and now find myself vaguely shamed to have not read the books. This nagging self-doubt had me launching into Plato's The Republic[3] some months back.

Sure, I realize and *appreciate* that this is a formative book for Western Civilization, and that the main players have largely defined the core elements of what I would consider a rational world-view, but man ... after reading this I *totally* understood why the Athenians wanted Socrates whacked!

Frankly, my expectations were probably tainted by my "text book excerpt" exposure, where the "significant bits" get highlighted, contextified, and discussed. This book, however, went on and on and on and on, and Socrates sure did seem to like to hear himself talk. My take-away from the "dynamics" of the book were that he was like a modern Rap star with his entourage, and would be playing to this particular audience of admirers who'd be responding primarily with the Ancient Greek version of *"tru dat!"* and *"yo! you da man, Socrates"*, etc. Needless to say, I'm glad I never had to write a paper on this as "A Blowhard and his Assembled Sycophants" (the latter term coming from Ancient Greek!), as that would have been something that would have likely had a negative impact on my admittedly, uh, "gentlemanly" GPA.

Once again, I had a bunch of small bookmarks in here that I have no idea now what I wanted to convey via (most were in the "politics" sections, so I might have been intending to comment on the unfortunate election of the

US's first ~~Communist~~ overtly Socialist government) ... so at least you're spared that rant.

Needless to say, there are *significant* parts to this book ... and it's one of those things that Should Be Read ... but the format is strange (imagine that in a book that's nearly two and a half millennia old, in a translation that was done over a century ago), and the ideas get chopped up into discussion fragments, and, well, it's *philosophy*.

So, if you don't want to go through life with this particular hole in *your* education, do by all means pick up a copy of The Republic[4] and make yourself read it. Heck, you might *like* it. One of the "happy things" about this "Dover Thrift Edition" is that it's a 320-page book with a cover price of just *$3.00*. It's in print, but good luck on getting your local brick-and-mortar to order it in for you (you figure the profit margin on this) ... so, your best bet is to keep it in mind for the next time your Amazon or B&N order is twenty-two bucks and you need something "small" to make it into the free-shipping promised land.

Notes:

1. http://btripp-books.livejournal.com/73480.html
2. http://btripp-books.com/
3-4. http://amzn.to/1WuowbV

Sunday, May 24, 2009[1]

A great book ...

I picked this up at the Newberry Library book sale last summer, and read it in October. It, unfortunately, got "backed up" when I hit a mental block on doing reviews and had languished in my to-be-reviewed pile for six months. This is particularly regrettable, as I was *quite* enthusiastic about the book when I finished it, and, obviously, a lot of that connection has faded with time.

Now, I am a rather fervent "antitheist" in that I feel that *religion* is A Bad Thing, despite having been a religion major, studied various traditions in depth, and have taken numerous initiations into several traditions. Christopher Hitchens rather summed up my take on Established Religion in his quote: *"Since it is obviously inconceivable that all religions can be right, the most reasonable conclusion is that they are all wrong."* ... and the more insistent that a particular Religion is that they "are the one true path" the more likely I am to consider them dangerously deluded.

However, my strong agnosticism has an open window for "experiential" spiritual paths, ones where the individual "works on themselves" and are verifiable within one's own being (like the Buddha said: *"Believe nothing ... unless it agrees with your own reason and your own common sense."*). This is, no doubt, why I found Swami Prabhavananda's Religion In Practice[2] so appealing, as it is not a *doctrinal* book, but a something of a guide for looking inside oneself (from a Vedanta perspective) and reaching out to the underlying spiritual realities.

This book, originally published in 1968, is a collection of talks that Prabhavananda gave at Vedanta Society locations in Southern California. There is a certain "going over the same points" in here due to this, as these talks were free-standing and not part of a course or curriculum. It has been assembled into five parts, "The Problem", "The Goal", "The Methods", "The Exemplars", and "Vital Questions on Religion Answered", each with various numbers of talks included. The most impressive part of this is "The Methods", which includes subject such as "Control of the Subconscious Mind", from which is this excerpt:

> ... owning to our different states of consciousness, we find that it is quite impossible to reach freedom, to reach God. In our waking state of consciousness, with our physical senses, with our human minds which can only become conscious of objects and things, we cannot reach that pure consciousness, however we may try. Then we go to sleep, we dream. There again, in the sleep of dreams, we cannot realize that pure consciousness. Then we go into deep sleep, we become unconscious; but, there is still a veil of darkness covering our consciousness. We do not realize pure consciousness.

> *So long as we live and move within these three states of consciousness, it is not possible to reach the realization of pure consciousness. We cannot see God, cannot realize God, within the provinces of these three states of consciousness that are known to us.*

He then goes on to discuss a "fourth state" of consciousness called Turiya[3], which is one of those concepts that I had managed to not encounter previous to reading this book.

I recall that when I finished reading Religion In Practice[4], I was wanting to go buy copies for my friends and family (I was *that* enthusiastic about it), but found, at first glance, that it was out of print. Certainly this version (the 1969 second printing hardcover) was out of print, and this is the only thing that Amazon has listed. However, with some additional digging, I discovered that this *is* being offered by Vedanta Press on their web site[5] in hardcover, new (I'm assuming), for the remarkably reasonable price of $8.95 ... which could explain why it's not out in Amazon or B&N (which take a very steep percentage, making it hard to sell low cover-priced books at anything other than a loss). While there are some copies floating around the used market, Vedanta Press may be your best bet on getting a hold of this. Needless to say, I'd recommend it to all and sundry!

Notes:

1. http://btripp-books.livejournal.com/73950.html
2. http://amzn.to/1TaL4In
3. https://en.wikipedia.org/wiki/Turiya
4. http://amzn.to/1TaL4In
5. https://www.vedanta.com/store/religion_in_practice.htm

Saturday, June 27, 2009[1]
Another ...

OK, so I was sort of mocking the "for dummies" books the last time I reviewed one, but here I am again, with another awaiting review! Frankly, I pretty much ordered Jerri Ledford's Google AdSense for Dummies[2] by mistake ... I have some projects where I'll be using Google's Ad Manager but the specific terminology was not set in my head when I went looking for something to get me up to speed with that, and saw books on Google's AdWords and this one on AdSense and figured this was the one I was looking for, only realizing after it arrived that it wasn't the "manual" that I was hoping to be reading. However, AdSense is a product that I'm likely to use at some point or another, so I figured "what the heck", and launched into it. This wasn't quite a quick a read as the Ning book (which I plowed through on one afternoon/evening), but that's because it wasn't something that was really holding my interest in the way that something that I was actually *working with* would have.

I don't generally read other reviews of a book before I write about it, but in this case I took a peek at the Amazon scribes and found *very* mixed reviews of it, some folks *savaging* it for perceived inaccuracies, some *raving* that it was a very useful introduction to the Google program. Having no functional experience with AdSense, I really couldn't speak to the accuracy of the book, but I found it informative, if a bit irritating in parts (the author appears to be some sort of religious fanatic and almost all her "examples" eventually got around to preachy sites).

Of course, the *sine qua non* of the "For Dummies" books is their ability to take the reader from total cluelessness to the ability to at least reasonably function in a program. Judged by this standard (and with the caveat that I haven't *tried* anything outlined in the book), I suspect that this fulfills its purpose, as I believe I have a pretty good sense of what's involved in running an AdSense campaign.

The most interesting parts of the book for me were on the "general website coaching" side of things ... recommendations of how to keep stuff fresh, how to incorporate profitable "key words" into your pages, and how to stay on the good side of Google (despite the many temptations out there that would lead you to the exile of the banned).

While I have had many web sites and blogs over the years (obviously, my main blogging platform is LiveJournal which does not offer ad options, so it's never been something I've thought at looking into except at the far end of having to make a massive content move to another service!), this at least gave me a context of what one might be able to produce off of one's sites. Honestly, none of my personal sites have ever had the sort of traffic that would make the effort involved (and resulting page clutter) worth the pennies that it might generate via a program like this, but this at least gives me some context from which to *discuss* the option with others whose sites I may be working on.

As is frequently the case, I got this via the new/used vendors on Amazon, with this running me a relatively high $8.42 (plus shipping) for a "new" copy, still a good discount from the $24.99 cover price and Amazon's own 34% discount. Given that the author has "tainted" the book with her religion (where it hardly belongs!), I'd wholeheartedly recommend getting this though the "used" channels (heck, the same vendor I got this from now has a "new" copy for just $3.79!) to deny her the revenue ... something that I usually feel genuinely bad about when pointing out the after-market option. I do feel, however, that this is a useful introduction if you're looking to make some change on your web sites.

Notes:

1. http://btripp-books.livejournal.com/74095.html
2. http://amzn.to/1TSnwua

Saturday, June 27, 2009[1]

A Classic?

I'm surprised that I hadn't read this one "back in the day" as this was the sort of book that would have easily fit into my late '70s and early '80s reading. I'd certainly been familiar with the *name*, but had never gotten around to picking up a copy until I encountered one at last summer's Newberry Library Book Fair.

The first thing that stands out about The Aquarian Gospel of Jesus the Christ[2] is its attribution simply "by Levi", which (with a little bit of Googling) turns out to be one Levi H. Dowling (1844-1911). When encountering "oddly named" authors one has to wonder what the story of the name is (some are simply fruitcakes, of course). In this case, I believe the author was at least trying to flag the book as having been "channeled". I had gotten about 20% into the book (which is set up like a Bible, with two columns a page of small sections, collected into larger sections, all numbered, etc.) and had one of those "what the *heck* is with this?" moments and went off to the Internet to fish up info.

It turns out that Mr. Dowling was a sort of fringe preacher who was enamored of (and I guess at least somewhat connected with) the Theosophists. I found this amusing, as my first thought was how much this sounded like Blavatsky's stuff from a similar period. However, rather than showing up in stacks of crayon-scrawled papers in the morning, Dowling directly set himself a program of "visualizations" which he claimed enabled him to "travel in time" and see the events of the past, in this case the life of Jesus.

The Aquarian Gospel[3] is probably best known for "filling in the missing years" of Jesus' history, that big gap that the Bible doesn't bother much with between "miraculous birth" and "ministry & death". According to Dowling, this information has now been "transcribed from the Akashic Records" ... good for us, eh?

The book is more-or-less in two parts ... the early years of John, Jesus' family, and "Jesus' travels", and then the standard New Testament stuff, retold. Frankly, the second half of the book is a real drag, as everybody knows the story, and Levi isn't adding much, just "spinning" things differently (notably, going out of his way to make Pontius Pilate look like a great guy) from the "usual version". The early part of the book is "the good stuff", with various teachers of John, Mary, other relatives, Jesus, etc., including transmuting "Abrahamic" religion into the "religion of Brahm", and relating that to various Persian and Indian (ala Brahma) cults and thence into Buddhism.

Eventually, Jesus "hits the road" and first spends a lot of time bouncing around India and interacting with the Hindu teachers ... inevitably, he gets on the wrong side of the priesthood and has to flee to Nepal, working with Buddhists, then to Tibet, and then back to India. From there he goes to Persia, Assyria, Chaldea, and Babylon before headed home just long enough for his mother to put on a big dinner for him and (I'm extrapolating here) do his laundry. The next stop is Greece, where he briefly hangs out with a guy called Apollo, and heaps tons on praise on the Greeks who weep when he leaves.

After Greece it's time for some schoolin' and the Aquarian Jesus is off to Egypt to study with the big boys ... the "Sacred Brotherhood" at the temple of Heliopolis. Here he passes through seven specific challenges, the last of which gives him the title of "The Christ". Passing this degree appears to have "changed the age" and the next thing is a meeting of "the seven sages of the world", conveniently all folks that Jesus was hanging out with in his various travels (who'da thunk?), in Alexandria.

Following this, the "standard" tale picks up again, albeit strongly flavored with Theosophical doctrine. The focus moves to John, then Jesus' early ministry, assembling his posse, and endearing himself to the mob while pissing off all sacred and temporal authority. You know the rest. The spin gets heavy after he's crucified, with a lot of "sacred brotherhood" stuff worthy of red and blue crayon, then dips back into the traditional story for Pentecost, and the book ends.

Frankly, as I struggled through the last half of the book, I wondered why this book didn't end up creating a cult of its own ... after all, this is "more canonical" than the Book of Mormon, and certainly no less wacky than Dianetics ... how come *those* went big-time and this stayed (while still in print a hundred years since its publication) on the sidelines? Must be not having a "huckster" to be pushing it ... Dowling died within 3 years of penning this, while Joseph Smith and L.Ron Hubbard were able to market the heck out of their books!

Anyway, as noted, this is still in print more than a century down the road, but, because of its vintage, it's also available free on the web[4] ... so if you want to check it out, it's only a few clicks away. Used copies (I got mine for $1.50 on "half-price Sunday" at Newberry), are available for as little as a buck forty-five in "good" condition via the Amazon new/used guys, so if you want a dead-tree version you might consider that, were this little bit of channeling something that you felt you couldn't go without.

Notes:

1. http://btripp-books.livejournal.com/74300.html
2-3. http://amzn.to/1VVn95A
4. http://www.sacred-texts.com/chr/agjc/index.htm

Sunday, June 28, 2009[1]

Hmmm ...

As I've probably detailed in this space previously, I encountered "The Enneagram" via Gurdjieff's work, which is, I believe, the ultimate source of all the current threads. However, most of what I've seen *outside* of "Fourth Way" teachings is some sort of half-baked fortune telling system, which has stripped away all the "difficult" parts of Gurdjieff's Enneagram, and left something of questionable use and doubtful validity. An example ... a number of years back I was at a networking event with a speaker, who was talking about how his consulting firm "worked with the Enneagram", and did a presentation of the watered-down variety. After his presentation I asked him "what about the *'outside shocks'*?", which are key elements in the Gurdjieff system ... it was clear that this fellow had *never heard* of the concept, and yet he and his organization were pitching themselves as experts!

So, it is with a certain trepidation that I approach any book on the subject of the Enneagram, as the "signal to noise" is getting more staticky every passing year. Unfortunately, Don Richard Riso's Understanding the Enneagram: The Practical Guide to Personality Types[2] does not disabuse me of the disdain I hold most of the works in this genre. You might well ask why I picked up this book ... and I can only say that it's been sitting around in the "to be read" boxes for nearly 20 years, was a book club edition, and probably seemed like a thing I'd enjoy reading back in the days when I could afford to buy books without a lot of discrimination!

In Riso's defense, his approach is not "newspaper horoscope", but neither does it take into account the *systemic* elements of Enneagram work. He all but admits the failings of this book, begging off on the *history* of the Enneagram, and on the "abstract theoretical aspects". Rather, he presents this as an expansion, and "practical guide" to the material he published in a previous book, *Personality Types*.

In this he deals with nine "personality types": 1 - The Reformer, 2 - The Helper, 3 - The Motivator, 4 - The Artist, 5 - The Thinker, 6 - The Loyalist, 7 - The Generalist, 8 - The Leader, and 9 - The Peacemaker. Each of these nine types are subject to "nine levels of development": 1 - Liberation, 2 - Psychological Capacity, 3 - Social Value, 4 - Imbalance, 5 - Interpersonal Control, 6 - Overcompensation, 7 - Violation, 8 - Delusion and Compulsion, and 9 - Pathological Destructiveness. This gives him 81 type/levels to play with in his descriptions. He also talks about "wings", sub-types on either side of one's "type", which (depending on dominance) provide a whole additional layer of combinations to write about. In addition to this there are "misidentifications" where somebody thinks they're one type when they're actually another, and how one type at one level can look like quite another type at some other level. Again, a lot of "stuff" but not necessarily very much "content".

While it ultimately might be on the level of your typical internet meme, the most *interesting* part of the book was the self-assessment questionnaire which is comprised of 20 "statements" for each of the 9 types, you go through and mark down which of these 180 items you "agree" or "strongly agree" with. Your main "type" should have fifteen or more of these. Interestingly, my results cooperated, with 17 for Type 5, 11 for Type 6, and 9 for Type 4, showing a primary type with its two "wings", while the others ranged from 1-6 (with a mean of 3). This suggests that Riso is perhaps onto *something*, although having my results pointing to "The Thinker" might be clouding my perceptions.

Again, I believe that Riso is *trying* to present something of value, but has "lost the key" in following the non-Gurdjieffian versions of the Enneagram work. I kept being frustrated by his "brushing off" the questions of *theory*, as I would have been more interested in reading about *that* than the various factors ("Childhood Origins", "Basic Fear", "Basic Desire", "Secondary Motivations", "Healthy Sense of Self", "Hidden Complaint", "Key Defense Mechanisms", "Characteristic Temptation", "Characteristic Vice", "Characteristic Virtue", and "Saving Grace") that he spins out for the various types here.

While I really can't *endorse* this book, it's also not the worst of its kind, and has its moments. I'd just have preferred reading the book that Riso says he can't write! If this sounds like something you'd be interested in, however, you're in luck as it can be had for cheap ... the Amazon new/used guys have "very good" copies for 1¢ and up, and "new" copies for as little as 58¢ (plus shipping, of course).

Notes:

1. http://btripp-books.livejournal.com/74686.html
2. http://amzn.to/24PrtF0

Sunday, June 28, 2009[1]

Wow ...

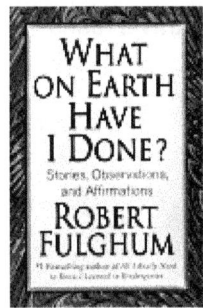

Every once in a while I will hit an absolute *gem* at the dollar store, and this is one of those times. I just finished this, and simply *had* to write about it before the glow wore off.

Now, I really wasn't familiar with Robert Fulghum, but I'd heard of some of his books (*All I Really Need To Know I Learned In Kindergarten*, etc.), still I launched into What On Earth Have I Done?: Stories, Observations, and Affirmations[2] with some caution, as I have a low tolerance to both preachy and syrupy books, and this, from the outside, held the possibility of being either or both of those. Fortunately, it was not.

I must admit, there was part of me (that frustrated writer whose sole outlet over the past decade or so has been blog scribblings) which was VERY envious of Fulghum's wandering lifestyle, spending part of the year in Seattle, part of it in Utah, and part of it in Crete (and parts elsewhere at conferences and such), and wondering how one gets to live that way on writing. Obviously, his "hook" is reaching out and touching his readers. Of course, he had a bit of a head start with me, being an older white guy, a UU minister, etc., hitting many trigger points for me to connect with him, but I really feel that his musings would effect other readers as strongly, although possibly for other reasons.

"Musings" is what I saw most of this book as. It appears that he writes (or at least wrote *this*) in sort of a journal, daily or weekly commentaries on things he thinks of, encounters, or recalls. Everything in it has a bit of a misty, dream-like characteristic, full of details but not hard and sharp in the telling. The book starts with the premise of "Mother Questions", *"What on Earth have you done?"*, *"What in the name of God are you doing?"*, *"What will you think of next?"*, and *"Who do you think you are?"*, which he turns around and asks of himself. I don't know if the rest of his books are as self-reflective as this, but it is a bit like finding a personal journal in a used book store and staring through it into the writer's soul.

From his telling, this Fulghum guy is a bit of a character, a trickster, a dreamer, a big kid, etc., and sounds like the type of guy I'd like to hang out with. He weaves in and out of social situations with a playful eye, being at least reasonably non-judgmental of those who don't care to play along. Perhaps most vividly, he paints a picture of the small town in Crete where he goes to write several months of the year, running off into several sidetracks about the history and personality of the place and people, probably to give a more vivid background for his stories of interactions there. Many of his tales are quite touching, especially the one about a highschool basketball coach, and his "secret weapon" ... which I won't spoil for you just in case you do pick this up!

What On Earth Have I Done?[3] is a *wonderful* book, and I highly recommend it to all and sundry. What is very strange (to me) is how this ended up *in the dollar store*. It still seems to be in print (Amazon has it at one of their standard discounts), and my copy even has a price sticker on the back that is *more* than the cover price of the book ($26.50 for a $22.95 edition) ... it's only been out a year and a half, and yet the new/used guys have "new" copies for as little as 36¢ so you *know* that something funky must be going on with the publisher. Anyway, if you can find it, get a copy ... I'm not sure I'd pay *retail* (although I'd hate to take away from the author's travel funds) for this, but it's a real treasure for the used/discontinued rate!

Notes:

1. http://btripp-books.livejournal.com/74973.html
2-3. http://amzn.to/1VVmK2U

Monday, June 29, 2009[1]

Fascinating ...

I have long had an interest in (and a taste for reading books on) the subject of a forgotten ancient civilization which pre-dates the "early" civilizations, and which might be the seed for these. This concept is, of course, *extremely* heretical in "official" circles, and the subject of both mocking and suppression. Yet the traces are there, from the megalithic ruins around the world to inexplicably detailed knowledge of things that "pre-historic" man had "no way of knowing".

In Civilization One: The World is Not as You Thought It Was[2] Christopher Knight and Alan Butler go on an intellectual journey of discovery in this shady backwater. The first concept that they put forth is one of "framing", calling it the "Great Wall Of History", which is traced out by the invention of writing in around 3,200 BCE and the "dawn of civilization" in places like Egypt and Sumer. However, *modern humans* go back at least 100,000 years, leaving a very, very long gap. The *homo sapiens* living 10,000 or 50,000 years ago were not much different from us today, yet because they are "on the other side of the wall" we (as a culture) dismiss them as "primitives".

There is a much bandied-about quote (frequently mis-attributed to various real-life personages, but actually coming from the pen of Ian Fleming via the Bond arch-villain Auric Goldfinger) which goes: "Once is happenstance. Twice is coincidence. Three times is enemy action." ... which keeps coming to mind while reading this book. Time and time again, the authors find situations where not only did "primitive" man seem to have measuring standards that were not only remarkably accurate, but are found again and again in cultures across the planet.

Much of this work starts with Prof. Alexander Thom's discovery of the "megalithic yard", a measure that figures repeatedly in the ancient stoneworks of the British Isles. A cube that is 1/10th of this yard will hold a pint of liquid, or a pound of grain ... remarkably preserved through folk custom in the UK (no wonder the English-speaking world has fought so much against the metric system and the Euro!). In fact, a whole spectrum of weights and measures relate to this one basic "yard".

This also relates to the Sumerian system of weights and measures, units of which fit remarkably with measurements of the size and weight *of the Earth*, and even of the speed of light(!). Now, I've not delved into this to check the math, but from what's presented in the book, there is "enemy action" all over the place, as "coincidence" hardly covers the fine-grained correspondences between what the *ancients* used for measure, and things that we currently know only from modern science.

The British Isles, Sumer, Egypt, Minoan Crete, ancient Japan, the same figures keep appearing, all which relate to the size of the Earth, the dynamics of the solar system, etc. ... it is fantastic stuff, but presented here as an unfolding of the authors' own search for answers. Frankly, they express constant disbelief in what they're finding, but again and again the numbers play out the same story.

Unlike theorists such as John Anthony West, the authors of Civilization One[3] do not necessarily posit a global antediluvian civilization, the stunned remnants of which crawled out of the ruins of a shattered world to re-boot culture along the banks of the Nile, the Tigris/Euphrates, and the Indus. Rather, in the closing chapters of this book, they drift towards the zone occupied by Zechariah Sitchin, taking the most ancient records *at their word* about super-humans that came from elsewhere ... teachers that brought knowledge to the scattered groups of humanity, and then left ... i.e. the "space alien" hypothesis. Given the deliberate pace and general caution exhibited through the course of the book, this must have been a very difficult conclusion to write!

Anyway, this is a fascinating read, and the level of "coincidence" of how the numbers work out on these widely-spread systems points to there being something well beyond that at the root of these traces. It's still in print if you want to check it out at your local brick-and-mortar book vendor, but the Amazon new/used vendors currently have it in "like new" condition for as little as $3.48 (plus shipping).

Notes:

1. http://btripp-books.livejournal.com/75069.html

2-3. http://amzn.to/24PqULj

Sunday, July 5, 2009[1]
When is a Goddess not a Goddess?

So, there I was, with a book that I needed to get from Amazon, and a good ways to go before I made it to the "free shipping" promised land. And, flipping through the suggestions, I notice a title that was familiar, and clicked on it. It was the right (discounted) price, and my order was good-to-go. Yep, that's the extent of the fore-thought and planning involved on my picking up Margaret Starbird's The Woman with the Alabaster Jar: Mary Magdalen and the Holy Grail[2] ... recognized the title from being referenced in other books of the "Holy Blood, Holy Grail" genre. I guess it's featured in *The DaVinci Code* as well (as the big starburst on the cover points out), but I've not gotten far enough from my "no fiction" ban to have been tempted to read anything that mass-market!

Personally, I found the *most interesting* thing about this book is its "back-story", of how the author, a one-time good Catholic girl (indeed, a RC theologian and university instructor), discovered the Baigent, Leigh, & Lincoln books and thought that they *just HAD to be wrong*, and set off to disprove the whole Jesus/Magdalen bloodline thing. And what happened? She found out that the *canonical* story was full of holes, that there was solid historical traces supporting the *heretical* version, and she suddenly is a major voice in the "goddess" movement, albeit in a quasi-Christian corner of it focusing on the Sarah (daughter of Jesus and Mary M.) lineage. It's mild sort of Schadenfreude, but I'll take it.

For those who have read widely in the genre, however, there isn't that much "new" in here, except, perhaps a deeper look into symbols in art and iconography which the author suggests are hidden signs of the Magdalen cult. Some of these seem a bit tenuous (i.e. any red X being a marker for the faith, no matter in what context), and some seem a bit stretched (almost anything appearing in a watermark: lions, unicorns, grapes, castles, crowns, etc., etc., etc.) ... here's a bit of a snippet along these lines:

> We have already established that the southern part of France was a seedbed for the Grail heresy and for the flowering of arts and letters during the twelfth century. The watermarks from Bayley's research throw a great deal of light on the faith of the heretics, who seem to have believed that Jesus was an earthen vessel for the spirit of God and that his teachings would lead them to personal enlightenment and transformation. Many also believed that Jesus was married and that his bloodline still flowed in the veins of certain of their Provençal families. Some of the watermarks were mystical, referring to the way of personal holiness, purification, and service to others outlined in the Gospels. Yet even these were heretical teachings because

> they bypassed the liturgies and sacraments of the established Church of Rome. Other watermarks wee heretical because they indicated a belief in a married Jesus who was the royal heir of David.

Again, this whole "watermark" thing seems a bit thin, but as "symbols" you can see where it played into Dan Brown's project. You can also see why the Church came down so hard on this region, perhaps being more bloodthirsty against the Cathars than they were against the Mohammedans!

There are bits and pieces in here which *are* fascinating, such as a famed 12th-century Magdalen painting *hanging in Ariel's Grotto* in the Disney version of *The Little Mermaid* (echoing themes of the Mediterranean coast of France, where mermaids can symbolize Mary/Sarah coming from the water), and traces of what *could* still be an organized movement (in fact, some threads in here weave in with parts of *The Sion Revelation* in a rather unexpected way). Starbird also dusts off her theological credentials and has a go at some rather substantial "reinterpretation" of chunks of the New Testament's Jesus stories, such as suggesting that "Mary and Joseph's flight into Egypt" was not Jesus' parents, but *his wife*, Mary Magdalen, accompanied by Joseph of Arimathea, who would later bring Mary and the young Sarah to France.

Of course, the underlying assumption here, that Jesus was *married* has certainly lost its shock value as book after book, looking into the culture of 1st century Palestine, point to the fact that *any* male of Jesus' age, and certainly one with "royal blood", would have been married from his late teens, if for nothing else than religious requirement. It was the emasculating of the Jewish Jesus by the Pauline Church that made it such a focus for the author, and that the figure of the Magdalen had survived the abuses of the Pauline re-boot is seen here as proof of her central role in the Jesus cult.

Anyway ... if you're a "babe in the woods" Christian and would like to have your eyes opened to some stuff that you might find amazing, The Woman with the Alabaster Jar[3] is almost a "must-read" for you. For those more familiar with the concepts here, it adds some material, but is not as strong a statement as one might like. This is available via the Amazon new/used guys for as little as a penny (plus $3.99 shipping, of course) for a "very good" copy, so if you feel like spending a few bucks on an interesting read, by all means do pick up one!

Notes:
1. http://btripp-books.livejournal.com/75390.html
2-3. http://amzn.to/223deed

Tuesday, July 7, 2009[1]

More ...

Some times things just work out ... in the previous book reviewed here, Henry Lincoln's The Holy Place: Discovering the Eighth Wonder of the Ancient World[2] was referenced several times, and I was surprised that I hadn't heard of it before. So off I went to Amazon, and was able to snag a used copy (it does appear to be out of print). As regular readers of this space may recall, I've read quite a lot in the Rennes-le-Château *genre* over the years, so I brought "a lot of baggage" to this book, which might not be fair to it. It is an *interesting* book in its focus on the place, but ...

The supposed topic of this book, "the Eighth Wonder of the Ancient World", is frustratingly hard to find within its pages. *Maddeningly* hard to find, especially given that the *end papers* of this hardcover edition are reproductions of detailed topographic maps of the region, but in such a scale that it's hard to even make out place names. If Lincoln and his publishers were able to get permission to USE these maps in the book, you would think they'd have done some of their graphing *on the maps*, but nooooooooo ... it's all pentagrams and hexagrams showing "straight lines" through places on blank paper. Lincoln posits that the whole region was one vast "temple", anchored at various points by churches, etc., but at NO POINT in the book are these diagrams and descriptions plotted against the maps, *which is supposedly how he discovered them*. Sure, this was published in 1991 (in that time before the Web), so we can forgive him not using Google satellite imagery (there is a great view of Rennes-le-Château there!), but how *blatant* a "tease" is it that he didn't reproduce the very evidence that led him to his premise?

Call me unimaginative, but I also have a very hard time with the whole "diagram on top of the text" thing. There is a very complicated, convoluted, and arcane cipher involved in part of this, and this is eventually "solved" (albeit with certain echoes of the "bible code" text crunching), why then start drawing stuff over it like you're going to come out of the exercise with a treasure map? I'm also much less impressed with "pentagrams" that are grossly distorted so that their points, intersects, and centers can fit over certain locations. Show me a *regular* figure that fits and I'll start thinking that maybe there's a "grand temple" there ... but I'm guessing that I could come up with just as good pentagrams by connecting Chicago suburbs on a map as what's presented here. Oh, yeah ... and *they're not shown on a map* so we pretty much have to take his word on it.

I hate to seem this irritated, but there is so much stuff *hinted at* in here that's just left hanging. Lincoln implies that there is a substantial pre-historic (or otherwise "lost") city sitting there waiting to be dug up at "Great Camp", among other things, only it's impossible to find these places, despite the enticing photos reproduced in the book.

Again, maybe it's *me*, but I find these carefully drawn out diagrams of 5, 6, even 10-pointed stars and various grids less than convincing when one considers how "random" the placement of landmarks appear to be on their lines ... and, as the book goes on, these keep getting bigger, more complicated, and including more "stuff".

You might be surprised to find that, despite all these caveats, I generally *liked* the book, and found much of the material quite engaging. It certainly puts the focus in on this one small (I was quite surprised to see what a tiny place Rennes-le-Château actually is) mountain village, and the countryside around it. It was fascinating to read of the possible pre-history of the area, hints of which come up in older ruins, and ruins incorporated into later structures. Of course, the whole "Magdalen" aspect is of interest as well. Ultimately, though, I don't feel *convinced* of the sub-titular premise ... it seems to me that Lincoln *could have* made a very substantial case by linking his various diagrams to topographic maps or aerial photography of the sites discussed ... trying to merge his descriptions and lay-outs to Google imagery seemed to go nowhere.

As noted, The Holy Place[3] appears to be out-of-print, so if you'd like to get a copy, you'll be in the hands of the used vendors ... however, this is available fairly reasonably (I got my copy for $2 plus shipping). While this suggests more questions than it answers, it certainly looks at aspects of the whole Priory of Sion mystery without bogging down in the more florid aspects of that story. This shouldn't be one's introduction to the subject, but if one has had some experience with the topic, it does have enticing bits to add.

Notes:

1. http://btripp-books.livejournal.com/75700.html
2-3. http://amzn.to/1XoiQPu

Wednesday, July 8, 2009[1]

Space ...

A while back I wrote a rather frustrated review of one of Paul Davies' books (a collection of lectures for a seminar) saying that nothing quite got where it needed to be going. Well, Cosmic Jackpot: Why Our Universe Is Just Right for Life[2] is the flip side of that coin, taking one of those themes and giving it a full examination.

Now, I have to admit that I had a trace of trepidation when picking up this book, as you never know where *fundie insanity* might raise its insufferable head, and one could certainly get the impression from the title/subtitle of this that it was nudging into "design" territory. Fortunately, this is not the case!

Of course, it can be argued that our particular Universe is *mighty* fine-tuned (at this particular point in time, in our particular point in space) to allow for the sort of observing creatures as humanity (as well as the other sentient biota of Earth), and Davies takes a good hard look at the number for many of the component parts of that.

As regular perusers of these reviews know, I've read *a lot* of books in this general genre, and so I'm always pleasantly surprised when I run across *something new* and this book did not disappoint with that. Among these was the remarkable assertion that the Universe has "zero mass", deriving from the argument that gravity is *negative energy* (in that one must apply *work* to counter gravity), and that if one totals up all the gravitational attraction, the number comes out very similar to the estimation of all the mass in the Universe! Cool, huh?

Davies looks at dark matter/energy, hidden dimensions, universal topography, the history of the Big Bang, and various theories, old and new. One point that Davies and I diverge on is the concept of the "Multiverse" ... he seems to be in the camp that feels that it is a philosophical slight-of-hand, where I still hold that it's the most *plausible* theory (that our Universe is only one among an infinity of other Universes, and the reason we're here to SEE this particular Universe is that it's one that happened to have "the settings" set for our particular type of creature, sort of a modified weak anthropic stance). He does take the "Multiverse" theory and spin off of it, however ... with one *fascinating* proposal ... in an "ultimate reality" of that sort, there should be "fake" Universes:

> ... if our universe is part of a multiverse, the balance of probability shifts dramatically in favor of simulation. It's a matter of basic statistics. ... the multiverse allows all possible variations on a theme, including [universes with a supercivilization with immense computational power] able to simulate fake realities. Unless there is some law that forbids emergence of such civilizations ... it is inevitable that some universes like ours will give rise to

> *universe-simulating supercivilizations. These universes will then spawn a vast number of fakes, so that in the total mix of real and fake universes, fake ones will overwhelmingly predominate. Therefore our universe is very, very likely to be a fake.*

Speaking as somebody who has spent much of the past couple of years working in Virtual Worlds, this does not seem too extreme a stretch ... because if we're able to produce immersive environments with our present technology, what could a people with many orders of magnitude more computing power than ours create?

Anyway, if you're interested in a solid, but not too technical, dip into the current state of cosmological theories ... you could do a lot worse than Cosmic Jackpot[3]. Davies covers most of the recent thought in the field with enough depth to give you familiarity, but not so much that you're spending all your time trying to wrap your head around the Calabi–Yau manifold[4] (a 6-dimension string topography)! This is still in print, so you should be able to find it at your larger local brick-and-mortar book vendors, however Amazon has it for 34% off of cover, and their new/used guys have "new" copies for as little as $1.41 ($5.40 with shipping). This is hardly a "for all and sundry" book, but if you'd be open to learning a lot about cosmology, I'd heartily endorse this.

Notes:

1. http://btripp-books.livejournal.com/75919.html

2-3. http://amzn.to/1rIAx0n

4. http://goo.gl/3KO8kW

Saturday, July 11, 2009[1]

Disappointing ...

This is one of those books which had developed a mystique around it in the years when it was out of print. As is (unfortunately) often the case, the reality of the book did not live up to the buzz. Charles Hapgood is an interesting character, having been a History professor, worked in the CIA, etc. Known best for his (quite excellent) *Maps of the Ancient Sea Kings*, he was willing to publish theories far off of the mainstream. The Path of the Pole[2] (a re-named second edition of his *The Earth's Shifting Crust*) is certainly in that zone.

There have been tantalizing bits of information out there regarding arctic discoveries of frozen megafauna (most notably Mammoths) with temperate climate spring/summer plant matter in their stomachs, and in some cases mouth/teeth (having been being chewed when the animal died). I've read of these in a number of books, and they certainly *suggest* a sudden shift of climate. I've also read other books which have traced out the "ice age" glaciations which neatly fit with a pattern of movement of the polar region in relation to the continents. This book is one of the seminal sources cited by many of these others, and yet ... this is only peripherally about that. Hap-good did not believe in continental drift (which, I take it, has been pretty much solidly accepted and understood in the half century since this book was first released), and sought an alternative theory to explain various phenomena. Perhaps one of the things that gives his theorizing so much weight is that he managed to get Albert Einstein to write a foreword to the first edition ... and while Einstein isn't "on board" with everything, he pretty much says "interesting stuff, should be researched". At the core of Hapgood's theory here is the concept that as ice builds up at the poles, the weight is "spun" towards the equator and causes crustal shifting and distortion, with volcanism, etc. resulting.

One of the most glaring "errors" here is his view of the Hawaiian islands. He keeps going back to them as an "anomaly", suggesting that the mass of these huge mountains should be distorting the crust under them. Needless to say, within the context of continental drift, it's clear that these were created by the Pacific plate moving over a "hot spot" with upwelling lava, building up each of the islands in the chain as it went. It was almost humorous to see him trying to calculate solutions to fit these with his theory.

Again, perhaps my expectations were misguided (I had really hoped that this would have discussed the previously-mentioned "pole shifts" resulting in the historic pattern of glaciation), but this book is more about an alternative theory to *continental drift* than being about movements of the pole. Given that Hapgood's underlying theories were incorrect, it's difficult to figure out what might be of use here. I've had numerous discussions with folks who totally reject polar shifting (for various physical reasons), but there are many things which would be "best explained" by this theory. Unfortunately, that's not what Hapgood was concerned with here.

The fact that Hapgood was not a PhD, and that his specialty was *history* and not *science*, come up from time to time in this. There are whole areas not approached here (such as the frequent flipping of the magnetic poles) which a specialist would have spent a considerable time with, and there is so much here that anybody who watches the science channels on cable TV would "know better" about, that it is frequently uncomfortable reading.

Still, there are some fascinating bits in this. Hapgood implies that South America has only very recently been "raised", with the area of Lake Titicaca (now at 12,500ft elevation) having at one point been at sea level, and tracing out "fossil shorelines" which indicate that the region is at a definite incline to the original water level. If one is to take the "conservative" estimates of the Tiwanaku (whose "harbor" features are currently fairly removed from the lake) ruins, this would mean that much of the uplift in the are has only been in the past 2,500 years (of course, these are "mainstream" dates for that culture, and not the "mystical" dates which would push that site into a far more ancient context).

Anyway, The Path of the Pole[3] goes a long way to prove what is unlikely to be provable, and is more embarrassing than interesting for most of it. While it has elements of the stuff I was hoping to read in it, they are incidental to Hapgood's main premise, a premise which is evidently incorrect. If you're still interested in it, it's still in print, and you might as well get it via Amazon (which has it for a discount, and available bundled with the far more satisfying *Maps of the Ancient Sea Kings* at just over the "free shipping" line). Frankly, I could have skipped this one, as it was a rather substantial read for a very minor pay-off.

Notes:
1. http://btripp-books.livejournal.com/76232.html
2-3 http://amzn.to/1ZKAmwg

Saturday, July 11, 2009[1]

Interesting ...

OK, so those of you who have been following this space with a "stalker-esque" attention to detail (comparing what's been coming through here with the record of my reading over on LibraryThing[2]) will know that I kind of got behind on my reviewing a number of months back, leaving me with a stack of books that were read between November '08 and February '09 still to be addressed. This is one of those. Needless to say, returning to a book six months or more after having read it is *not* the most ideal context for writing a review (the books hardly being "fresh" in my thought stream), and for this I apologize. So, if some of the upcoming reviews are a bit more "mechanical" than usual, please don't quit reading thinking "I've lost it" as I work my way through the backlog!

Those regulars will know that I've read many books in "alternative Biblical interpretation" (to give a "big tent" name to a number of associated genres), and Hugh J. Schonfield's The Passover Plot[3] is certainly among that part of my library. The tone of this one, however, is rather different, rather than trying to re-write the *theological* base of Christianity, it takes a more "investigative" look at the stories and what, realistically, was likely to have been behind them. As one could guess from the title, Schonfield's conclusion is something of a well-planned conspiracy aimed at an actual Messianic kingship for Jesus, hatched by him and certain key associates.

This is not to say that the book doesn't have something of a theological axe to grind, the failings and hypocrisies of Christianity are frequently pointed out:

> The Christian message obtained the most recruits among the slaves and underprivileged. Many of them, as we find in Paul's letters, were not only of low morality, but factious, restless and disaffected.
> ...
> The message about Jesus found a lodging among peoples who believed in the commerce of gods with mortals and were accustomed to the deification of rulers and other outstanding personages. ...
> There is a widespread desire for a realistic rather than an idealized representation of Jesus. The Traditional portraiture no longer satisfies: it is too baffling in its apparent contradiction of the terms of our earthly existence. The God-man of Christianity is increasingly incredible, yet it is not easy to break with centuries of authoritative instruction and devout faith, and there remains embedded deep in the sub-conscious a strong sense of the supernatural inherited from remote ages. ...

> The modern dilemma of Christianity is patent and stems from a creed which down the centuries has so insisted on seeing God in Jesus Christ that it is in danger, as is now evident, of being unable to apprehend the existence of God without him. Far too many Christians do not know God in any other way than through Jesus. Take away the deity of Jesus and their faith in God is imperiled or destroyed. The New Testament is not entirely to be blamed for this. The major fault lies with those who have pandered to the ignorance and superstition of the people in giving them a God created in the image of man.

So, ultimately, what the author attempts here is to strip away the "superstition", and get to a view of the realistic, human, and historical milieu in which these individuals acted. In this, much of the book unfolds like a TV "procedural" looking at events and trying to pry out of the descriptions a likely 1st century scenario. Much of this hinges on peripheral (yet recurring) characters from the biblical narrative, and positing that some of these were closer to "the inner circle" than the "big name" apostles. To give one example: when folks are sent ahead to get an ass for Jesus' entry into Jerusalem (carefully adhering to the Old Testament "script") it's not a *miracle* that the animal is just where Jesus tells them to look, or that the owner allows them to take it when told a particular phrase, these sorts of things have all been pre-set to allow the mythic elements to accrue to Jesus.

It would appear that the timing, situations, and activities all point to a plan to have Jesus *suffer* on the cross, but not to *die* there (the crucifixion coming so close to the sundown on the Sabbath, when his associates could beg for the body, not being a coincidence), however the "piercing of the side" seems to have complicated things, and, rather than rising to reestablish the Jewish Theocracy, Jesus dies and leaves his followers at loose ends.

The book is in two parts, the stuff leading up to the crucifixion, and the stuff that ended up coagulating into Christianity after the crucifixion. There is a lot of very interesting evidence brought forth for both sides, but way too much to even sketch out here. Needless to say, The Passover Plot[4] is a fascinating read, and I'd highly recommend it to anybody looking to make sense of the generally absurd Christian religion! It is still in print, and has a very low cover price, so this is one that you might as well grab at your local brick-and-mortar book vendor (Amazon has a minor discount on it, and their used guys aren't much lower than that when you figure in shipping). It's not a "light" read, but is nonetheless very illuminating!

Notes:

1. http://btripp-books.livejournal.com/76293.html

2. http://btripp-books.com/

3-4. http://amzn.to/24TvxaL

Saturday, July 11, 2009[1]
Well, the price was right ...

This was another dollar store find. Again, I wonder what the dynamic is that lands pristine hard-cover books which are in general retail circulation there at a buck, but I try not to "look a gift horse in the mouth", and I'm really more picky than one might think from my reviews (there were three "plausible" books there today that I just wasn't motivated to read at the moment) in what I'll get there.

The "self-help" genre is *not* a major factor in my library (despite several recent entries), and, while I recognized the titles of the author's previous mega-sellers, I'd certainly never actually *read* them. Richard Carlson, Ph.D., is the "Small Stuff" guy, which gives some context to the title What About the Big Stuff?: Finding Strength and Moving Forward When the Stakes Are High[2], this being his look at getting through the "crunchy" parts of life (and, as anybody who reads my main journal knows, I'm going through one of those right now financially, so hoped to "pick up some pointers" for fending off the depression of joblessness in this).

I wonder, however, who "his audience" is ... I was never able to "connect" here (unlike that Robert Fulghum book of a couple of weeks back) and even the "to the point" entries of the several dozen in here seemed to be at a distance. This had a disjointed feel (to me) like tuning into a TV program that one had never seen and never heard of and having to figure out what was happening, where the characters were coming from, etc. Carlson never grounds this in his own existence (although he references his experiences frequently), and it's like he's approaching each of the sections from some randomly selected stance, one quasi-Sufi, one quasi-Buddhist, most fairly new-agey. It was a bit of a "curveball" when late in the book he starts talking about his having attended a Christian university, as his vibe up to that point was definitely not of the "preachy" variety! Perhaps he's writing for the great grey mass out there who never get particularly reflective, nor have spiritual training beyond the basic Sunday School rhetoric to help guide them through life's challenges, but the over-all impression I got from this was that it was "tepid", and while his suggestions for various situations were well-considered they were (for somebody who has read widely) a bit like suggesting that one put a band-aid on a cut, or a lotion on a burn.

There are forty sections here, which tackle (to quote from the dust jacket) *"the difficult issues - from illness, death, injury and aging, to alcoholism, divorce, and financial pressures - with his trademark wise and eminently helpful advice"*. Again, there is nothing that jumped up here and started to trigger the B.S. sensors (well *"wise and eminently helpful"* came close) but there was also nothing that stood out and made me say (in the words of the late great Johnny Carson) "I *did not* know that!" ... and, as finding new stuff is one of my main pleasures of reading, this proved to make this something of a disappointment.

Of course, I return to the fact that this isn't my genre of choice. There are plenty of folks out there who would no doubt find this an *inspirational* book, but it just never connected for me, although, as noted, it's all "useful" advice. I do have one personal issue with this, however (not that all the preceding couldn't be taken as "personal issues"), I found that in reading this I kept spinning *into* depressive states ... but perhaps that's on me and my current situation (it could happen reading the Sports pages, I guess), and not so much on the book, but it was definitely triggering stuff for me (and not in a *constructive* way).

Needless to say (although I did so in the post's title) the price was right on What About the Big Stuff?[3] for me (via the dollar store) ... if you want a copy, you're going to have to shell out more than that, although the Amazon new/used vendors do have "new" copies for as little as a penny (well, $4 with shipping). Oddly, there is a substantial discrepancy between the "cover price" on the copy I have ($19.95) and the "cover price" that Amazon (and BN) list ($27.95) ... I would not recommend paying either of those for this, of course!

Notes:

1. http://btripp-books.livejournal.com/76604.html

2-3. http://amzn.to/1rIzMUP

Sunday, July 12, 2009[1]
But, you've read this one already ...

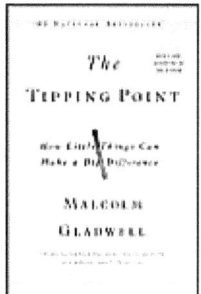

This is another of the books that has languished in my "yet to be reviewed" pile for several months, oddly in that I was quite enthusiastic about it, but it was something that just didn't say "write about me!" when I blocked out time for reviewing. In reflection on this, one thing does occur to me. Just as my reading over the past decade has included very little fiction, I've also steered away, as much as possible, from "popular" books ... anything (as this does) trumpeting being a "#1 National Bestseller" being of questionable value for my limited reading time (as the gist of it will no doubt "filter through" various media channels whether I want it to or not).

While I'd heard of the book (the title being something of a buzzword for a while there), the first I really "encountered" Malcolm Gladwell's The Tipping Point: How Little Things Can Make a Big Difference[2] was via my old Toastmasters group, where one member was quite enamored of the stories in it, and spun off a number of his speeches from these. I also had another personal connection with this book, albeit in a second-hand and inconvenient manner. One of the subjects of one of the chapters here had been featured in a magazine story that I'd encountered on the web. She was the head of a Department in the City of Chicago, lived in my neighborhood, and was likely to have certain acquaintances in common with me ... and was featured as one of those people who just *knew everybody*. As I was, at the time (as I am now), in a rather desperate job search, I attempted to connect with this person, hoping that she could point me towards some likely places where I could find employment. Unfortunately, due to having been featured in this book (a fact I was unaware of when writing to her), she gets hundreds of such requests a week, and is unable to respond to any of these (I was so informed by her assistant). So, the book, when I got around to reading it, was ever so slightly *tainted* by this experience!

The over-all premise here (as one might infer from the subtitle) is that there are small things, seemingly insignificant on their own, which can produce rather substantial changes in the world (much like the classic "butterfly wing" adage in relation to weather patterns). The book looks at various topics: crime (the "broken window" theory, Bernie Goetz, etc.), marketing (from shoes to books, etc.), health, education, and communications, bringing in examples of how certain things filter through certain people in certain ways and then explode on the general consciousness.

One of the most fascinating things in here is "the magic number one hundred and fifty", 150 being the approximate number of individuals that any given human is really able to have a social relationship with. One researcher has an equation that relates the size of the neocortex to a "social relation" number, and it appears to work quite well across all the great apes (including us). Interestingly, the 150 group size crops up over and over again in human history, from typical village development to church size in certain denominations, to effective unit size in the military.

Concepts slide back and forth within the sections of The Tipping Point[3], as definitions of people functioning as "connectors, mavens, and salesmen" have applications in almost every one of these, and "stickiness" can apply as well to both *Sesame Street* and cigarettes. There are many amazing research studies referenced here, from the classic "six degrees of separation" work of Milgram in the 60's to work done in TV and direct marketing. Overall the book frames a "new way" of thinking about the world, although not presenting itself in that light. One thing the book does *not* do is to formalize this ... frankly, there is enough material and structure in this to make up a good solid minor cult (think of the crap that's grown up around the Enneagram), and I don't know if I'm relieved or disappointed that there isn't (to my knowledge) a "Tipping Point School" out there!

This is, of course, still in print (and no doubt easy to find at your local brick-and-mortar book vendor), but Amazon has this paperback at a whopping 43% off of cover (putting it well under ten bucks), which puts it on a par with the cheapest of the used options (w/shipping). This is certainly one of those that I would recommend to anybody interested in how human consciousness (especially in social settings) works.

Notes:

1. http://btripp-books.livejournal.com/77024.html
2-3. http://amzn.to/1X57S14

Sunday, July 12, 2009[1]
A bit deeper into the stack ...

As I've noted, I'm trying to catch up on a fairly large stack of "to be reviewed" books going back as far as last fall. This one's been waiting since December, so my impressions are somewhat dulled by the delay, but I'll have a go at it.

I picked this up at used book store a year or so back, and the copy I have *looks* considerably older than it is ... this came out in 1997. I make a point of this, as I tried to do some follow-up research on a couple of things which grabbed my imagination at the time of reading, but I was singularly unable to find any current vestiges of those programs and projects that I was seeking more info on. There appears to have been a second edition of this (at least Amazon defaults to a different cover), but that appears to have just been a couple of years after this one, so I doubt that is more current at this point. This is too bad, because Janine M. Benyus' Biomimicry: Innovation Inspired by Nature[2] is based on a fascinating concept; *Biomimicry* is defined here as 1) a new science that studies nature's models and then imitates or takes inspiration from these designs and processes to solve human problems (e.g. a solar cell inspired by a leaf), 2) a method that uses an ecological standard to judge the "rightness" of our innovations - after 3.8 billion years of evolution has learned what works, what is appropriate, and what lasts, and 3) a new way of viewing and valuing nature which introduces a model based not on what we can *extract* from the natural world, but on what we can *learn* from it.

The book is in 8 chapters, an introductory one and then seven which seek to answer certain questions ... How Will We Feed Ourselves? - Farming To Fit The Land: Growing Food Like A Prairie ... How Will We Harness Energy? - Light Into Life: Gathering Energy Like A Leaf ... How Will We Make Things? - Fitting Form To Function: Weaving Fibers Like A Spider ... How Will We Heal Ourselves? - Experts In Our Midst: Finding Cures Like A Chimp ... How Will We Store What We Learn? - Dances With Molecules: Computing Like A Cell ... How Will We Conduct Business? - Closing The Loops In Commerce: Running A Business Like A Redwood Forest ... and Where Will We Go From Here? - May Wonders Never Cease: Toward A Biomimetic Future. As you can tell from reading over that list, the book covers a lot of ground, some being more "Biomimetic" than others, and some being *more plausible* than others. Frankly, I wanted to run off to Kansas after reading about The Land Institute as what Benyus wrote about them was deeply inspiring ... she also covers a half a dozen other renewable resource approaches from around the world in that chapter (from fish to wood to low-impact farming).

However, some stuff in here is pretty stale ... the computer-themed section goes back more than a dozen years, and stuff that seemed "gee wiz" back then has long been lapped (try telling somebody in the mid-90's that a Terabyte external hard drive would be the size of a book and cost less than a nice dinner for two) by reality ... plus there's a lot of "guessing" about things like "holographic storage" which so far has remained within the realm of fiction. And, needless to say, when you start getting Gaia referenced in the "Running A Business" section, you know that you're in territory only reasonable to the Green Party loons.

All in all, though, Biomimicry[3] is a pretty thought-provoking read, although frustrating for the reasons detailed above. It appears that this is currently out of print, so if you're interested in picking up a copy, you'll be at the mercy of the new/used vendors ... oddly enough, the hardcover version of the first edition is probably your best bet, with "like new" copies going for as little as $7.50 (where some guys are trying to sell "new" copies of the later paperback for upwards of seventy bucks!) ... or, you could find it in a used bookstore like I did.

Notes:

1. http://btripp-books.livejournal.com/77112.html
2-3. http://amzn.to/1rIz8GQ

Monday, July 13, 2009[1]

Puh-leeze ...

Further into the "to be reviewed" pile ... this one's been waiting for about six months. As you might guess, The Subversive Imagination: Artists, Society & Social Responsibility[2] (edited by Carol Becker) came from one of my previous used bookstore hauls, as it's hardly the sort of thing that I would have made a point of buying, but looked interesting enough to add to a shopping bag that was getting filled for a flat rate!

This is one of those books that give Academics a bad name. Most of society does not think like this. And, even in 1994, this book is spewing re-hashed Marxist dialectics dealing with ascending and declining classes, utilitarian and decadent art, and *the proletariat* and *the bourgeoisie* ... it's depressing that there are people so out of touch with reality that they still cling to that sort of crap. I lay this at the doorstep of Academia as this is clearly a *text book*, as the "native audience" for this kind of sludge is hardly sufficient to have kept it in print for 15 years, plus the cover price is $34.95 (for a book shy of 300 pages), a sure sign that it's being forced down the throats of relatively captive consumers.

The book is set up in three sections, "Personal Responsibility and Political Contingencies", "Decolonizing the Imagination", and "Theorizing the Future", having seven, five, and three essays respectively from a wide assortment of writers, who are (for the most part) purported to be artists, but are mainly focused on Politics and "culture war" in various contexts and locations around the globe.

As personally distasteful the unavoidable Leftist stance of this book is, I will credit with containing several quite engaging narratives. *Of course* they're all "anti-American", "anti-White", and "anti-Western", but some open up windows into places and things that might not be accessible otherwise. Perhaps the most fascinating is Felipe Ehrenberg's telling of a story about the origin of the "bark paintings of Guerrero", which, rather than being a "traditional craft" evolved within the writer's life from a style used for ceramic figures ... and I can attest to the ubiquitous presence of the "bark paintings" in nearly every Mexico City tchotchke shop! There is also a very interesting piece about Salman Rushdie which features more Leftist self-reflection that I'm used to seeing.

Anyway, if you're of the Ward Churchill camp, you'll *love* The Subversive Imagination[3]. I think everybody else will find it irritating, if interesting in parts. As noted above, this is (incredibly) still in print, if at a grossly inflated price. Amazon has it at a whopping 10% off, and the new/used guys have "good" paperback copies for as low as $7.99 (plus shipping). I would have been pissed to have paid more than the 25¢ that this cost me (it was from that "fill a shopping bag for $5" fund-raiser I wrote about a year or two back), so I can't really recommend you part with the dollars!

Notes:
1. http://btripp-books.livejournal.com/77337.html
2. http://amzn.to/1X55UO4

Saturday, July 18, 2009[1]
There's no place like home, there's no place like home ...

I have to admit upfront on this, that there is *no way* that I can write an "unbiased" review of Love, Sex, Fear, Death: The Inside Story of The Process Church of the Final Judgment[2] by Timothy Wyllie (and others). The Process/Foundation was a key element in my development as person, and it's almost like having to write a review about a book about one's *parents* ... how does one take *that* step back?

When I was a lad, we lived one block away from the Process center in Chicago, and, following "the Schism", the Foundation's HQ was a scant few blocks from my high school. Over the years, I came to know many of the folks out "donating" (selling magazines to raise money) on the streets, and came very, *very* close to "joining the cult" rather than going to college. I could go into a whole array of stories here (I stayed in on-going communication with them all through college, and in intermittent contact beyond), but that would only be digressing from the book.

In many ways, Love, Sex, Fear, Death[3] seems to have been seeded by Genesis P-Orridge who put together Wyllie with the Feral House publishing folks. GPO has had a long-time fascination with the Process Church, which has expressed itself in various forms (and collaborations) over the years.

Frankly, I rather expect that this book will be followed by a raft of others. The Process and Foundation had been very tightly controlled (or, at least the upper parts of their hierarchies) by Mary Ann DeGrimston (nee MacLean), the one-time wife of the titular head and "Teacher" of the Process, Robert DeGrimston (Moore) ... "the Matriarch" died a few years back, and this has evidently changed the nature of "the game". To some extent, this has freed up people to be more open about the organization and its history, although I'm not certain on what *level* that freeing has come.

Timothy Wyllie had been one of the "inner core" from the very beginning, going back to when Robert and Mary Ann left the structure of early Scientology (due to a philosophical disagreement over the work of Adler) and started their own group called Compulsions Analysis. In fact, Wyllie reports that he'd volunteered to be a "test subject" for them from the get-go, so there are few with as "deep roots" in the organization. In the church he was called Father Micah, and was the person behind the "look and feel" of the classic Process magazines (the title of the book appears to be a bit of a joke spun from the subjects of the last 4 "themed" issues of The Process, which actually came out in the order: Sex, Fear, Death, Love), elements of which are reproduced in a section of color plates here.

I actually became *involved* with the group soon after "The Schism" (when Robert was removed as Teacher, the theology and symbology changed, and about 2/3rds of the group continued on as The Foundation) and their previous incarnation as The Process was very much something Not To Be Discussed. Being the inquisitive (and obsessive-compulsive) lad that I am, I kept digging, and eventually had both a pretty good picture of the general outlines of the history, but also quite a respectable collection old magazines, books, and pamphlets. Of course, I was still just "peeking through holes in the fence" and had very little idea of the non-mythologized history of the group ... Love, Sex, Fear, Death[4] finally fills in a lot of the gaps.

The key thing about the Process/Foundation was that, to a very great extent, the *people* involved were all very much like me ... highly intelligent misfits who were out of step with society (aka *"the grey forces"*) in general. I never felt *more at home* than the times I was out in New York, and hanging around the big HQ on 1st Avenue (some summers I'd go out there three times). This part of the story comes rather late in Wyllie's section of the book (which includes remembrances from a handful of other members, as well as an essay by GPO), but it was *fascinating* to be able to read an "insider's view" of that time.

In many ways, the book was a somewhat depressing read for me, having had an inner mythology of the Process/Foundation that ran in parallel with the *official* mythology, neither of which came particularly close to the realities outlined by Wyllie. The "real" Process/Foundation sounds like a very difficult place to have been, and in some ways I came away from this book feeling a certain level of *relief* that I had never taken the step to "go in". I also had a few revelations regarding certain aspects of things which, in context, do not reflect well upon some people for whom I've always held the highest regard.

Of course, this is a book by *somebody who left*. Fr. Micah (Wyllie) did not continue with the group after New York (when they sold the HQ to buy the Kanab Movie Ranch). This was a huge change for the group, and I have one story that I think I will tell. If you've ever seen the (wonderful) movie *Where The Buffalo Roam* with Bill Murray playing Hunter S. Thompson, there's a scene where Lazlo (his lawyer) talks his way onto the press plane and corners HST with a briefcase full of 8x10 B&W photos of desert, trying to convince him that this would be some sort of paradise. Two of my closest connections with the group made a regular "funding" trip out to Chicago every year, and I was sitting in somebody's living room when one of them cornered *me* with 8x10 B&W photos of desert, and proceeded to explain how this was going to be some sort of paradise ... it was a deeply weird moment for me. Some years later, I actually found myself "in the neighborhood" (Flagstaff, AZ) with a couple of days to kill, and drove up to visit. The area is very beautiful, but it was very strange to be seeing adult people who I had last seen as young kids, and once-edgy young people now well into middle age or beyond!

The point I was getting to (before the seemingly inevitable digression above) is that I will be very interested to see if folks who *did* venture out west and transform into Best Friends Animal Sanctuary will now be able (or even inclined) to write their own histories. There have been losses among the inner core (one of my closer friends from that group died tragically a few years back), but quite a number of those who came together in the early 60's are still around, and it would be *fascinating* if they collectively, or individually, would produce clear-eyed histories from their perspectives.

Of course, Love, Sex, Fear, Death[5] is not "for everyone" ... I can well imagine that many people could not care less about a small, if notorious, religious group from the 60's and 70's (despite their rather broad, if subtle, influence on popular culture over the past forty years), but for me this is a blockbuster book, full of insights and revelations about people I *knew*, places *I'd been*, and, heck, (if I'm not grossly mistaken) I just missed being "name checked" in GPO's essay! So, while I'd really *love* to have all and sundry run out and buy a copy, I'll understand if your enthusiasm for this is not quite up to mine. As this is a brand-new release (it officially came out on June 1st), you can no doubt find it anywhere, but Amazon has it at 34% off of cover, which is a pretty good deal.

I think on some level I'm feeling that *"the more people read this book, the more people will understand me"*, which is somewhat pitiful, but the whole Process/Foundation "thing" is something that I've had to explain and explain and explain over the years, and it's nice to have something out there that's shedding some light on the subject while not "sensationalizing" it!

Notes:

1. http://btripp-books.livejournal.com/77773.html
2-5. http://amzn.to/1ZKv03Z

Saturday, July 18, 2009[1]

Ah ... Feynman ...

One is tempted to say that "in the world of physics" there are very few figures like Richard P. Feynman, but when you think about it, in *general* there are very few like him. Both brilliant and irreverent, Feynman cut a swath through his environment, often exasperating his more-staid colleagues (as when he made a hobby of "cracking" top-secret safes while working on the Manhattan Project), but also charming the public (how many other theoretical physicists promulgated guides for picking up Vegas showgirls?).

QED: The Strange Theory of Light and Matter[2] is a collection of four lectures where he seeks to explain, to a non-specialist audience, the theory of Quantum Electrodynamics (for which he'd been given the Nobel Prize). The circumstances of these lectures are worth noting, as Feynman had a wide circle of friends, one couple (of means) had funded a series of lectures and invited Feynman to launch the series with the four in this book (which came five years before his death in 1988).

The four lectures here are titled "Introduction" (which faked me out, as I was expecting a few pages of intro, but this runs a quarter of the book!), "Photons: Particles of Light", "Electrons and Their Interactions", and "Loose Ends", and in them Feynman takes the reader through an increasingly challenging information curve (I admit, he did manage to "lose me" at a couple of points towards the end). Feynman warns the listener/reader early on, saying *"What I am going to tell you about is what we teach our physics students in the third or fourth year of graduate school – and you think I'm going to explain it to you so you can understand it?"*. Of course, despite my passing familiarity with the topic, I had issues with parts of it (albeit not the concept of the "absurdity of Nature"), but I also had some of those much-treasured "AHA!" moments where he clarifies something that I knew *of*, but did not fully "get".

Prime among these revelations was the "inner workings" of the basic Feynman Diagrams. I had encountered these in various contexts over the years, and understood that they represented visualizations of how particles can exchange, emit, and absorb other particles as they move through space/time (even, arguably, backwards in time). I had never known, however, the ways these were specifically drawn out. One of the first things that Feynman deals with here is how those lines are developed, with a "clock hand" that spins at different rates depending on the particle and its vibration (i.e., pure blue light's dial "spins" faster than pure red light). Each of these produces a reading which involves length and direction, and all possible states for an event are calculated, and a resulting arrow created. Needless to say, this can become very complicated!

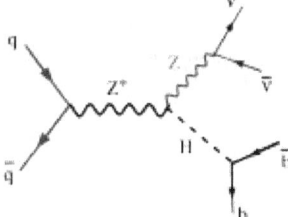

Feynman Diagram

Of course, one of the most endearing aspects to Dr. Feynman was his wry humor ... which helps to sugar-coat many difficult concepts here. I thought I'd share at least one, and had found this particularly amusing as I was reading through the book:

> There was also the problem of what holds the neutrons and protons together inside the nucleus. It was realized right away that it could not be the exchange of photons, because the forces holding the nucleus together were much stronger – the energy required to break up a nucleus is much greater that that required to knock an electron away from an atom in the same proportion that an atomic bomb is more destructive than dynamite: exploding dynamite is a rearrangement of the electron patterns, while an exploding atomic bomb is a rearrangement of the proton-neutron patterns.

... doesn't it sound so simple when put that way?

Anyway, this does appear to be in print (and, judging from the numbers of copies held on LibraryThing[3], I'm guessing that the "Princeton Science Library" edition is used as a textbook), so, should you have a burning desire to come to a fresh appreciation of the inner workings of nature (at least to the extent that Quantum Electrodynamics describes them), it should be easy enough to find a copy. Amazon has it at a very reasonable 32% discount from (a very reasonable) cover price, which is only slightly bettered by the new/used guys (after shipping, of course). Again, I realize that reading physics for relaxation is not most folks' first choice, so I won't *insist* that your intellectual development is not complete without this, but do consider picking up *some* Feynman (*"Surely You're Joking..."* is probably a much better introduction to the man and his thought anyway) to familiarize yourself with one of the most amazing humans to have graced the planet!

Notes:

1. http://btripp-books.livejournal.com/78009.html
2. http://amzn.to/221m1gA
3. http://btripp-books.com/

Saturday, July 18, 2009[1]
Metaphysics by committee?

I feel that I need to apologize to whatever readers there are out there for these reviews because I'm getting to this book eight months after having finished reading it. Needless to say, with that sort of delay, my impressions are somewhat vague as to the details. I do recall, however, that I was having a *very* hard time "getting the right angle" to approach this book. The subject, the chapter headings, the *concept* all sounded *great*, but there was never any "payoff", and I was finding it difficult to adequately express that. The triumvirate that penned God and the Evolving Universe: The Next Step in Personal Evolution[2] *should* have been able to produce a fascinating book. Over time I have developed a grudging respect for James Redfield (of the *Celestine* books), due to the inclusion of rather high-level Incan Shamanic practices (albeit not presented as such) in his books, and one would think that Michael Murphy (co-founder of the Esalen Institute) would bring a lot to the table ... I don't know anything about Sylvia Timbers, but I suspect she's *not* the factor dragging this down. My #1 "take away" from this was that they never *got* anywhere in it.

This was very much like a movie where it's all "backstory", pointing towards the place the tale is supposed to go, but never getting there. It was a very frustrating read as one would launch into a chapter thinking "OK, now we're getting somewhere" and it would just be another "backgrounder" about stuff that may or may not be out there. Towards the end there seemed to be some effort to try to steer the book into something that would at least resemble what was "promised" in its title/subtitle, but it felt like a patch job. In retrospect, this seems like it could very well have been three folks with a lot of "dribs and drabs" they'd written on various New Age subjects pulling together their files and trying to justify a book out of that material.

I had bookmarked some sections to use in this, but they'd be more of a tease than anything, as (while there are some worthwhile subjects raised here) nothing gets beyond the *"gee, what if THIS happened?"* sort of drivel. To give you a sense, however, of what's in here, let me walk you through the "structure". Part One - Awakening: 1) The Mystery of Our Being, 2) A History of Human Awakening; Part Two - The Emerging Human Being: 3) Our Expanding Perception, 4) The Mystery of Movement, 5) Enhancing Communication, 6) Opening to a Greater Energy, 7) Ecstasy, 8) Love, 9) Transcendent Identity, 10) Transcendent Knowing, 11) A Will Beyond Ego, 12) The Experience of Integration and Synchronistic Flow; Part Three - Participating: 13) Transforming Culture, 14) The Afterlife and Angelic Realms, 15) Luminous Embodiment; Part Four - Practices and Readings: 16) Transformative Practice, 17) A Guide to the Literature of Transformation.

Of course, I have an extremely low tolerance for "fluffy bunny" Newagism, so the vast lot of the ooohing and aaahing involved here over rather flimsy bits of wishful thinking does not draw me in at all. As noted, the main reaction I had to this was that "there was no *there* there".

This is another case where I'm willing to indulge in a bit of *Schadenfreude* in feeling a certain amount of satisfaction that this is, despite its big name authors, out of print just a few years since its publication! However, their loss could be your, well, "gain" isn't necessarily the best word for it, but if you (for some inexplicable reason) found this to be something that you just *had* to read, you could find "very good" copies available from the Amazon new/used guys for as little as a penny (plus shipping, of course), and "new" copies for about a buck and a half. Personally, I wouldn't recommend you wasting time on it, but (in the words of the late Johnny Carson) "It takes all types to fill the freeway".

Notes:

1. http://btripp-books.livejournal.com/78158.html
2. http://amzn.to/22lI1cl

Monday, July 20, 2009[1]

Great political memoir ...

For those of you playing along at home, I'm *almost* caught up with getting reviews done for the big stack of books that had built up here ... I just have three left to go, and they're all political, and they're all pretty "stale" at this point ... this one having waited nearly nine months for me to getting around to it. While I have general *impressions* of this from when I read it, the details have faded a bit, so I'm going to be fairly cursory on this.

Never Again: Securing America and Restoring Justice[2] is something of a "political memoir" by former Attorney General John Ashcroft ... while having certain solid *opinions*, this book doesn't have a particular "axe to grind", and follows through several years (from Ashcroft losing his Senate seat to a *deceased* opponent to his resigning the A.G. office due to poor health) of some of the most tumultuous history the country has ever known.

Of course, the "elephant in the room" throughout the book, and what spurs the title, was the attacks of September 11th, 2001, but that is just one aspect of this, the efforts around that are interwoven with many other crises and challenges that Ashcroft had to face.

Not surprising, one of the main challenges he had was trying to resurrect the Justice Department after it had devolved into a subsidiary of the Clinton "dirty tricks" operation under Janet Reno. The festering morass of the Clinton regime (which created "the wall" between the CIA and the FBI to prevent the FBI getting wind of all the under-the-table cash deals that had been going down between the White House and the PRC) is dealt with in shocking detail in the early parts of this, with the horror show of the very people (Jamie Gorelick, etc.) who had *intentionally crippled* our intelligence services during the Clinton regime ending up on the "9/11 Commission"!

Of course, this is Ashcroft's version of the events, so I guess it's not surprising that the reader comes away with a bit of "heroic vision" of the man, but in the course of reading this my opinions of him shifted from *ambivalent* (having absorbed some of the unrelenting left-wing attacks from the media) to quite admiring his service to the country. However, I suspect that liberals and leftists of various stripes would, were they even *able* to pick up the book, have a total freak-out over it.

The writing here is pretty solid (not a given for a political book), and the "pacing" is pretty good. Needless to say, there was a lot of *drama* over the "Ashcroft years", so the subject matter doesn't need much "punching up". It provides a very interesting window into the G.W. Bush administration, and counters many of the "general knowledge" lies the Media has put out there about those years. I can only hope that THIS will be the historical view of the era, and not the deliberate propaganda campaign the execrable MSM spewed out for the previous eight years!

I am happy to report that Never Again[3] is still in print, although I got my copy at the dollar store. It's a bit pricey for what it is ... there are "new" copies, however, available from the Amazon new/used vendors for as little as 1¢ ($4.00 with shipping), so that would be my recommendation, unless you're feeling *real* flush and wanting to make sure Mr. Ashcroft gets his royalties. Again, I very much *enjoyed* this book, but I suspect that the extent that you will love or hate it falls very much on how you feel on Clinton/Bush and Reno/Ashcroft scales!

Notes:

1. http://btripp-books.livejournal.com/78501.html
2. http://amzn.to/1WsAlPU

Tuesday, July 21, 2009[1]
A dream destroyed ...

OK, I'm down to the last *two* books left from that stack of backed-up things to review, and both of these share certain aspects, so these will go back-to-back with similar messages.

Three years. That's how long it took *this* book to go from an impassioned call to action to being a sad reflection of what might have been. In Painting the Map Red: The Fight to Create a Permanent Republican Majority[2] Hugh Hewitt charts out a very plausible strategy for the GOP to wrest back control of the Congress ... plausible in a "more perfect world". Unfortunately, the Republicans were being Democrats, the Democrats were being Stalinists, and the MSM was completely stacking the deck. Rather than "take back" Congress, of course, the Republicans lost more seats, setting up the present ugly scenario of an ultra-left Legislature supporting a dictatorial Executive with wet dreams of being another Castro, Chavez, or perhaps even Pol Pot. The author is prophetic when he says:

> It may be that the radical left will take the Democratic Party back to power in the House, the Senate, the presidency, or all three. If that happens the country ought to have been given fair warning of the nature of the government they will receive under those circumstances.

... how sad that nobody in the GOP heeded this warning, and the voters handed the machinery of oppression to the likes of Pelosi, Reid, and Obama.

Hewitt advises the GOP to press through five messages, that the Leftist Democrats have declared war on the military, that they've declared war on religion, that they've declared war on the Judiciary, that they're wanting to radically re-define marriage, and that they're "addicted to venom", while blaming it all on the Republicans. Sound familiar? That could be the Cliffs' Notes for the past three years. Needless to say, the GOP did not manage to make a peep on any of this, while RINOs like Bush and McCain tried to "play nice" with the Democrats. He warns them that this is a recipe for disaster, that the GOP has to "stand for something", but instead there was Bush trying to "reach across the aisle" to the vipers who took a mile for every inch he offered, and McCain, who never should have had an (R) next to his name in the first place!

Again, looking back from 2009, this all sounds so *naive* for the 2006 midterm elections. Between the far left of the Democratic party and the total collusion of the main stream media, along with the deer-in-the-headlights approach of the GOP, this country went from "iffy" to "Hell" in 3 short years. Reading this now just rips at the gut, two Congressional elections and one disastrous Presidential race down the road. It's a vision of a better world that is likely now the stuff of myth, unretrievable in the new nightmare reality.

What's amazing about Painting the Map Red[3] (which I picked up, in hardcover, from the dollar store) is that it's still in print (and for a hefty sum, at that). However, if you want to see what *should have been done* prior to the 2006 Congressional elections, you can get this in "like new" condition from the Amazon new/used guys for as little as a penny (or four bucks with shipping). Hewitt raises a lot of good points in here, but it reads like instructions for latching the barn door after the tornado has blown through and destroyed everything. I suppose it's worth a read, but it's the sort of thing that makes a sane man want a whole raft of stiff drinks.

Notes:

1. http://btripp-books.livejournal.com/78661.html

2-3. http://amzn.to/1T9ZQo2

Wednesday, July 22, 2009[1]
Brilliant ... if not for that "imaginary friend" stuff ...

So, I know that those of you on the wrong side of the right/left line will already have your panties in a knot just from looking at the book cover, but I'm still going to write the review. If you're getting a wedgie from the thought of the guy *being allowed to write*, go off and watch one of your Michael Moore videos and you'll feel better.

For the rest of you, let me say up front that Newt Gingrich's Winning The Future: A 21st Century Contract with America[2] is a frustrating book for me, on a number of levels. Like the Hewitt book I just got done writing about, this (dating from 2005) has the same *"we can fix this"* hopefulness, while clearly pointing out the hazards on the horizon. From the current place on the other side of the Socialist over-throw of America, this is a sad read.

There is also, unfortunately, the whole "vague theocracy" in Gingrich's unsubtle religious focus which is the fulcrum point of many, if not most, of his arguments, making it hard for folks like me to fully get behind him. I can only imagine what a Hell the *likes* of Thomas Paine would consider the USA in a time when the choices go down to Pelosi/Obama on one side and Gingrich/Bush on the other. Why can't there be a "sane center" that rejects delusional fairy tales of both Marxism and Religion???

Only the ACORN-types (who will lie about *anything* if it suits their political ends) would deny that Gingrich is a brilliant political thinker, and here's he's best when he's discussing things like "Bringing The Courts Back Under The Constitution", or "A 21st Century Intelligent Health System". The book is all over the map, however, warning of dire results of not "changing" our approaches to many things: Social Security, Immigration, Education, Global Economy, Science, Technology, Energy, etc. ... in each case Gingrich presents a very perceptive analysis of what is wrong, what is possible, and what ought to be done for moving the country forward, in nearly every case pushing entrepreneurial solutions and reduction of government.

Like *that's* ever going to happen again. Now in the "nightmare time" all this rings hollow, hopes for *freedom*, personal responsibility, traditional American values ... things that the Leftist juggernaut is fast making impossible for any to reclaim, for generations, if not centuries.

The one point where Gingrich FAILS is that he seems to believe that the values that Paine laid out in *The Age of Reason* (not specifically, of course, but speaking in general of "American Values") originated in some *Christian* context. This level of cognitive disconnect always amazes me, as those who conceived America were, at best, ambivalent about organized religion, and in many cases hostile to it. This book would be a magnificent document if Newt had just left the random religious drivel out of it.

Anyway, living in our current dystopian descent, Winning The Future[3] offers little but a bittersweet vision of what could have been, had the past decade played out according to a different script. Once again, I found this hardcover edition at the dollar store, but it appears to still be in print. Fortunately (were you to want to torture yourself with fading visions of America), this can be had from the new/used guys for as little as 1¢ for a "very good" and 4¢ for a "like new" copy (plus the $3.99 shipping, of course). At this point, in these dark days, given the caveats above, I'm not sure I can really *recommend* this, but it is quite an inspiring vision of "what could have been" had the U.S. not gone to Hell in a handbasket.

Notes:

1. http://btripp-books.livejournal.com/78999.html

2. http://amzn.to/1T9ZqOB

Saturday, July 25, 2009[1]

Some amazing stuff ...

While reading this, I was repeatedly *quite enthused* about the material it was presenting, even to the point where I was considering *scanning* a particular chapter to send off to certain friends. However, now that I've *finished* it, I'm sort of drawing a blank about what to *say* about it here ... odd.

I'm not sure what specifically spurred me to order Lynn McTaggart's The Intention Experiment: Using Your Thoughts to Change Your Life and the World[2], although I'm guessing that I saw it referenced in something else (but I don't have a clue what that would be at this point). That would explain why I'd have picked up *this* rather than her previous book (on which a good deal of this is based), *The Field*, which has languished on my Amazon wishlist for quite a while ... oh, well.

The first thing that most people seem to notice about The Intention Experiment[3], once they've finished it, is that it's not very much about any specific program of experimentation, despite the cover announcing that one can *"Take Part in the World's Largest Mind-over-Matter Experiment"*. Only the last 15% of the book is *about* the "experiment" (which is on-going at the author's site[4]), with the preceding 85% of the book being a review of previous experiments in the area of consciousness' effects on various systems. Now, this is *not a complaint* ... the most fascinating parts of this book are her in-depth research into all the pre-existing (and, generally speaking, very minimally reported otherwise) work that's been done in this area, it's just that the book would leave the reader "more satisfied", perhaps, had it been titled *Towards A Program Of Intention Experimentation*!

Maybe one of the reasons I'm having such a hard time getting a hand on reviewing this, is that there is *so much stuff* in here. It's structured into four sections of four chapters each, with "The Science of Intention" (my favorite part of the book), "Powering Up" (dealing with setting, timing, location, etc.), "The Power of Your Thoughts" (including some amazing things about positive vs. negative prayer, and temporal issues), and the final bit about the author's on-going project. I was, frankly, somewhat amazed at just how much "good" work has been done in this area ... tests where dozens of variables are being accounted for, solidly devised double-blind trials, etc., and key scales for measuring effectiveness (which are often an order of magnitude greater than what passes for "effective" in drugs).

Now, I've been kicking around in "metaphysical" circles for well over 30 years, and I've seen and heard a lot of stuff in that time, and I was constantly being reminded of various things from my past while reading this, such as a Shamanic teacher insisting that one use some sort of a focused motion when working with energy, which has its parallel in a particular study reported in here, and a further expression in an examination of certain martial arts. Needless to say, these sorts of things kept grabbing my attention. Again, there is so much material covered here that it's very difficult to even mention particulars without spinning into a greater length than this needs to be.

One area that I found quite interesting (no doubt because I hadn't encountered it previously) was the work in "biophoton emissions", where all living systems *give off light* (albeit a few photons here and there, picked up by a CCD camera system), which serves as a theoretical basis on how assorted "organizing systems" can coordinate within and between living things. This then plays into the whole "quantum weirdness" realm, with waves, entanglement, and unexpected temporal functions.

Oh, yes ... that's one of the stranger sets of experiments here. Sending intention *backwards in time* to seek to effect experiments previously done. In these, some system (there were various examples) has elements of it recorded where frequency, or symmetry, or some other quantifiable factor is measured (say, for example, something happening on the left of a recorder or on the right). The record of this was then "shelved" for a period of time, and later an experiment was run where people would try to "send intention" about a non-average result happening (say, more clicks on the left than on the right, when the experiment *should* be right around even). The tapes are then examined, and *voilà*, there's an effect ... bringing you right around into "Schrodinger's Cat" territory pointing towards *consciousness* and observation *creating* reality.

And, isn't that what all this "Intention" stuff is about, after all? That one can *create one's reality*? As I suggested, this book takes a strange path to get where it's going, but the ride's interesting, and at the end, it's pretty open ... as one can run off to the web site and immerse oneself in additional projects and materials.

From my perspective, the weakest part of this was in the part intended to get folks ready to work on this, "The Intention Exercises", which seemed alternately newagey-preachy and simultaneously overly basic *and* a bit scattered. However, I'm guessing that there was a committee involved in that and they were trying to be all things to all readers/associates.

Needless to say, I'd highly recommend The Intention Experiment[5] to all and sundry ... and if you have *any* interest in the science of consciousness, this is quite a great resource (if just for the 20+ page bibliography). It's in print, so you could find it at your local brick-and-mortar book vendor (at a very reasonable cover price), but Amazon has it at just over ten bucks (which is better, if you get the order up to "free shipping", than what the new/used guys have it for with their flat rate shipping). Again, the only negatives here are the oddly minimal inclusion of the title subject, and a slight "newagey" spin to things once the author starts talking about *her* stuff, but these are minor blemishes on what is otherwise a *fascinating* book!

Notes:

1..http://btripp-books.livejournal.com/79284.html

2-3. http://amzn.to/1OpUX2Y

4. http://theintentionexperiment.com/

5. http://amzn.to/1OpUX2Y

Thursday, July 30, 2009[1]
Stuff I didn't know about ...

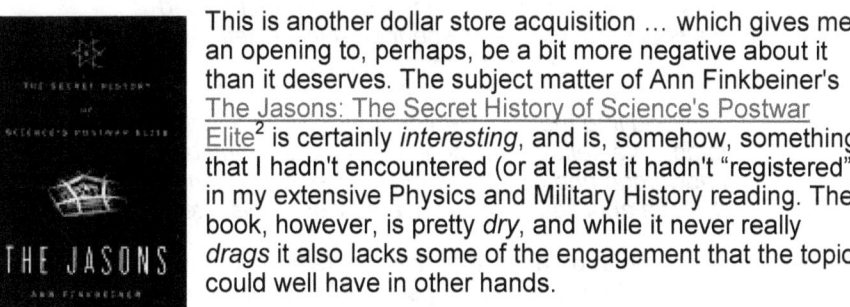

This is another dollar store acquisition ... which gives me an opening to, perhaps, be a bit more negative about it than it deserves. The subject matter of Ann Finkbeiner's The Jasons: The Secret History of Science's Postwar Elite[2] is certainly *interesting*, and is, somehow, something that I hadn't encountered (or at least it hadn't "registered") in my extensive Physics and Military History reading. The book, however, is pretty *dry*, and while it never really *drags* it also lacks some of the engagement that the topic could well have in other hands.

"The Jasons" were a loose grouping of top-notch scientists (initially primarily Physicists), which were assembled to help the Government with various projects, working on particular problems over a several-week session in the summer each year, starting in the thick of the Cold War. Initially named Project 137 (an in-joke for the denominator of the fine structure constant), the group first met in 1958, scant months after the Soviet launch of Sputnik. This was largely the "next generation" down from the Manhattan Project crowd, young, brilliant, and eager to tackle serious science problems. At first they were simply being briefed by the military regarding general challenges that were proving difficult to solve, from communicating with submarines, to improving the still-nascent US satellite program. The name "Jason" seems to have come from the wife of one of the initial group, although the specifics are blurred with time (the suggestion is that they were like Jason seeking the Golden Fleece).

I don't know where the fault lies in this book, the "science stories" involved could have had the vibrancy of a "procedural" thriller, but more focus seems to have gone to the moral status of the various teams over time. The author does not appear to be inclined to "flesh out" scenarios that she does not have primary or secondary source material for, so there is less narrative than one might prefer in this sort of a history, she is very much limited by what the various participants (and their associates) are willing (or, for security reasons, able) to discuss with her. And it appears that, to a certain extent, many of the older members (this book came out in 2006, nearly 50 years after the first group of "Jasons" met) were more willing to reflect on their *feeling* about their work with Jason rather than "juicy details" of the work itself.

It is also possible that Finkbeiner had "an axe to grind" here, as the subject of campus resistance to the U.S. Military in the 60's and 70's, keeps getting interjected, and one suspects that she might have a bit more than passing sympathy for the anti-war cause. She makes an effort in the early chapters (echoed on the dust jacket) to create a "philosophical" basis for the book:

> The idea that curiosity leads to disaster has an ancient pedigree. Pandora opened the gods' box and let loose all the evils of the world; the descendants of Noah built the Tower of Babel to reach heaven,

> but God scattered them and confounded their language; Icarus flew so close to the sun that his homemade wings melted, and he fell into the sea and drowned; Eve at the apple of knowledge and was exiled from the Garden of Eden; Faust traded his soul for sorcery and spent eternity in Hell. Saint Augustine , along with most medieval Christian theologians, considered **curiositas** a vice. The idea survived into the twentieth century about halfway intact. We believe that curiosity is the beginning of knowledge and especially of science, but we know that the application of science has led to disaster.

This sets the book up to be a morality tale, but (aside from the reports of various interactions of the participating scientists) there's not enough "there" there to make that work either.

So, while this is an interesting reporting of a fascinating project, it neither "delivers the goods" as a science history, nor as a grand moral struggle. Throw in the heavy sprinkling of passing references to the politics and politicians inter-relating with the Jasons, and the whole becomes weaker than the details involved.

As I so often end up saying, the above doesn't mean that The Jasons[3] is a *bad* book, only that it could have been so much *more*, whether as a scientific saga, a baby-boom bile fest, or even as a political tale. As it is, it's a bit of each, and is lessened in its lack of focus. Needless to say, I would have *preferred* a book that went more into the research and scientific discovery, but (as noted above) some of this stuff is still *classified*, so would have posed serious challenges to flesh this out as much as I would have liked in that direction!

Again, this book is only 3 years old and is already out of print, so I guess there weren't many who found this to their liking. As mentioned, I found it at the dollar store, so you might be able to find a copy similarly discounted, and the Amazon new/used guys have "good" copies for as low as a penny (plus S&H, natch), and "like new" for a couple of bucks. Once more, this is a *flawed* book (it had all the signs of an interesting project that only became untenable far too down the line to scrap it altogether), but not a *bad* book, and it's written *well enough* that it doesn't get noticeably bogged down at any point. If you're interested in physics, politics, and military history (all at once) this is likely a good book for you, with lessening degrees of likelihood depending on the mix of those interests.

Notes:
1. http://btripp-books.livejournal.com/79544.html
2-3. http://amzn.to/1Oly5Xq

Thursday, July 30, 2009[1]
Very odd ...

Yes, I know that I *frequently* describe assorted books here as "odd", but this one is *quite* odd in that, while it does *appear* to have an ISBN and a publisher, there is no trace of this on the Internet ... not at Amazon, not at B&N, not on LibraryThing.com, not in the various corners poked into by Google. And, this isn't some obscure chapbook from the 1960's ... it was published just four years ago, not in some unpronounceable place in south or central Asia, but right here in the U.S. of A., so there is no good reason that this should be so *invisible*! How did I get it? The author (and his associates from http://iamprakash.com*) had a table at a recent "sidewalk sale" up in Lincoln Square, and they *gave* me a couple of books, this being one of them. Very odd, indeed.

This slim volume, *Almost Home: A Correspondence with a Spiritual Teacher*, is fairly odd in and of itself. It is not directly attributed to a particular author (although "Prakash" is on the spine), and appears to be an actual set of e-mail exchanges between "Angie" and "Prakash" (aka Kevin Edwards). Now, Prakash, as one might guess from the name, is a bit of a New Age teacher. Frankly, what I've read of his writing so far has impressed me with its focus, directness, and ecumenical sourcing. So, I was somewhat surprised to find that the main credential that he trots out is "a Masters Degree in Sacred Theology from the *Angelicum* in Rome", which, upon a bit more digging, is *not* some new age workshop space in the back of a coffeehouse, but The Pontifical University of Saint Thomas Aquinas, brought to you by the same lovely Dominican order that was so zealous with their management of the Inquisition!

In this book, "Angie" (who appears to be a real person, but her web site is locked down, and there's not much else about her) is going for a mid-life Confirmation in the Catholic Church (a conversion, I take it), and she is having all sorts of cognitive dissonance (OK, she doesn't see it that way, just "weakness") with all the B.S. that's involved with trying to swallow The Big Lie lock, stock, and barrel. I guess Prakash (based on his Dominican training?) was recommended to her and they have this back-and-forth exchange.

As noted above, there is *nothing* that I could find any fault with (well, the Biblical references, but that's just *me*) in anything that Prakash tells her ... but it's almost comical to watch "Angie" fall all over herself trying to out-Catholic the Pope, interspersed with "oh, now I'm *enlightened!*" non-sequiturs of the newage variety. Prakash is obviously very well versed in Buddhism, Vedanta, Sufism, etc. and brings this awareness to bear on the floundering "Angie". The book takes her through almost a "deprogramming" and then into a "Catholic relapse". I suspect that the reason this book is "invisible" is that "Angie" (who does have a full name listed) decided that full-bore Papism was what she needed rather than enlightenment, and pulled out of the project (speaking of "projects", the apparent publisher of this is a group called "Awakened Heart Project" which is the name of a newagey *Jewish* site, but with no mention of this book). This could explain the sort of "shadow existence" the book seems to be in at this point!

Anyway, I am fascinated by this Prakash fellow ... I'm presently reading the other book I got from them, and am quite taken by his substance and style (as opposed to the videos on his site, which, frankly, creep me out a bit) ... I will be interested in figuring out what he's about and where he's coming from. Again, *his side* of these exchanges are quite inspiring, and well worth the read.

Since there is no "trace" of *Almost Home* out in the real world, it appears that ordering it direct is one's only option ... it is available there, as is a .pdf download of about 1/4th of the book (interesting, with the ISBN stripped out). *{NOTE: the site for the book has since disappeared from the web.*}* This is an odd one, but the "teaching" in it seems to be quality, so you might want to check it out (I think I will have something more substantial to say about the next one!).

Notes:

1. http://btripp-books.livejournal.com/79729.html

* Since writing this review, the only connection to this book that I could find on the web, the web site http://iamprakash.com/ has evidently been "lost" to the author and re-used by some design company. Remarkably, there doesn't seem to be a trace of it on Amazon or any other book site, aside from those related to my review. There is another book by "Kevin Edwards (Prakash)" on Amazon, a few links to classes he did at yoga centers about a decade ago, plus a number of interviews, etc. on Russian sites ... but, unfortunately, nothing that would connect you with a copy of this book.

Sunday, August 2, 2009[1]

The other ...

This is the other book by Prakash (although going by his "real name" here) that I got the other day. Every now and again I hit one of these "meditational" books and realize that *my* reading habits and the *book's* structure are just going to be in conflict. I *plow through* books, and some really ought to be read in dribs and drabs. This one, for instance, is comprised of about 140 "lessons" which would likely be best approached by reading one in the morning or at night and rolling it around in one's head for a day before moving on to the next one. Unfortunately, the structure here meant that it was just a "quick read" for me, with many of the subtleties involved in the individual chapters (most a single page or less) no doubt blurring as I sped by.

Kevin Edwards' The Master: Parables For Enlightenment[2] is certainly easier to *find* than his "Almost Home" book, being on LibraryThing.com[3], and available (if only via the new/used guys) on Amazon, and one wonders "what the story is" on the different situations on the two books. Like the other, there is a good deal of quality material here, but in a somewhat odd format. This is set up a bit like a collection of wisdom stories from a "Master", although the situations (and gender) of "The Master" keeps changing. While not all the sections specifically conform to it, each is, generally speaking, comprised of a title, a paragraph-long "parable", some brief statement related to the story, and then a quote from some notable source. I don't know why, specifically, but the tone here reminds me of Thich Nhat Hanh's writings. Anyway, here's an excerpt that I (for some reason) found particularly clarifying:

The Movers

* After making every conceivable effort to move the odd-shaped desk through the doorway, the movers decided to take it apart. Within seconds, they dismantled the desk and carried it through with ease.

As a skilled mover takes apart furniture to move freely through the doorway, a wise man dismantles beliefs to pass easily through life.

* * *

Every time you make sense out of reality, you bump into something that destroys the sense you made.
Antony De Mello

Now, obviously, this one doesn't have "The Master" figuring into the story line (even as narrator), but this is the way most of these play out, with story-saying-quote being the pattern of most of these. The quotes come mainly (about 1/3rd of them) from The Bible, but the rest range from Hafiz to Eleanor Roosevelt, and from the Buddha to Voltaire.

Again, this would probably prove the *most valuable* to one if one was taking it nice and slowly and "savoring" the small readings here on a daily basis. Obviously, the form of the structure is intended to give the reader several "angles" on a particular problem, which then allows a certain triangulation on the "truth" involved. As noted in my previous review, this Kevin Edwards "Prakash" fellow seems to have a lot of knowing at his command, but I'm still somewhat questioning what he's specifically about. His writing has a delightful and effortless eclecticism about it, but I do find his "Dominican roots" (his main credential seems to have been from the "Angelicum" in Rome, which turns out to be a "Pontifical University" connected to the Vatican!) somewhat troubling. His "Enter The New" program appears to be based, however, in Vedanta concepts, and he certainly is well versed in various forms of Buddhist thought as well, so I'm suspecting that he's not a "closet inquisitioner' (but, then again, *"**Nobody** expects the Spanish Inquisition!"*).

While The Master[4] *can* be found via the "usual channels", your best bet might be via Edward's website, http://iamprakash.com {NOTE: this is no longer his site} ... which also has more info on his other projects. I always feel somewhat churlish to be pointing readers off to "cheaper" sources of the books I review here when I've been *given* them by the author, but the Amazon "aftermarket" guys do have new copies of this for a very reasonable price (and Amazon proper does not seem to be specifically carrying it, even though bn.com does have it available). As noted, I wish I had more of a "dossier" on place the author's coming from, but I've been impressed with his vision, and would certainly recommend his books if you're looking for something a bit more meaty than simply "inspirational" in a metaphysical read.

Notes:

1. http://btripp-books.livejournal.com/79940.html
2. http://amzn.to/24H3bAs
3. http://btripp-books.com/
4. http://amzn.to/24H3bAs

Tuesday, August 4, 2009[1]
Long, long time ago ...

Civilizations of the
Indus Valley and
Beyond Sir Mortimer Wheeler

There was a time, some 30-odd years ago, when I was thinking that I was going to be an Archaeologist. "Stuff happened" and this did not come to pass, but I was *fascinated* with the dawn of Civilization, and especially with the Indus Valley cities like Mohenjo-Daro. So, I was quite pleased when I found (at the Newberry Library's Book Fair a week or so back) a copy of Sir Mortimer Wheeler's Civilizations of the Indus Valley and Beyond[2]. As it has been quite a while since I specifically dealt with any of this, I'm not sure if the Indus Valley has yielded up more data since this came out (my interest in the area was flowering in the late '70s), but this is a 1972 re-print of the 1966 edition, so there's been nearly a half-century in which significant work could have been produced, and the combination of that time with my own detachment from the subject leaves me in a place where (without doing a bunch of additional research) I really can't say whether Wheeler's material is "current" or long surpassed. However, as I see (thanks Wikipedia!) that archaeological work was halted in the area in 1965 (I suppose that the Pakistanis share the Taliban's hatred of any pre-Islamic cultural artifacts), most of what's in here is what's out there.

This book is quite extensively illustrated (in a mid-60's way), which lets one "armchair travel" to these sites. What is fascinating about the Indus Valley civilization is that it pretty much just *appeared* about 2,600 BCE with a whole series of cities (one, Harappa has given its name to the culture as "Harappan", but the city itself was the victim of "pragmatic looters", the workers on the railway opted to use the bricks of Harappa as a base for the rails rather than make their own!) along the Indus. These do not appear to have "evolved" in the sense that a city like Paris or London built up from its smaller predecessors, but arrived fully-grown, with a sophisticated grid system of streets, grain storage facilities, and (most remarkably) an advanced sanitation system of toilets, sewers, and drainage. Needless to say, city planning, advanced engineering, specialized architecture needs to come from *somewhere* and the lack of evident antecedents to the Indus Valley culture is one of the great mysteries (I had a theory, but it plays more to the writing of John Anthony West than to "standard" archaeology).

The book is, however, only partially about this culture, and it looks at surrounding areas, and then runs the timeline up through the Greek and Persian phases. Wheeler seems to tip-toe around the "Aryan invasion", not being willing to assign specific archaeological finds to this event, but he *does* note that some rather grisly discoveries (massacred bodies left as they fell) may well be a result of that historical influx, as some of the cities seem to correspond to places mentioned in the (Aryan) Rigveda. There is a bit of a gap between the decline of the Harappan culture (the theory seems to be that there was a seismic event sometime around 1900 BCE which caused significant re-channeling of the rivers and a substantial change in the local climate which led to this downfall) and the arrival of the Aryan tribes, but the fall of the former may well have opened the door for the latter, and residual populations may have still been in the remnants of the great cities by that time.

Remarkably, for a book this old (which is out of print) there are "very good" copies available of Civilizations of the Indus Valley and Beyond[3] via the new/used vendors, for as little as $3.58 (plus shipping). Of course, you might find a copy like I did (on the half-off day at the Newberry), but if you're interested in the subject, this is a very nice, and remarkably *readable* introduction. As a side note, the copy I got had an "ex libris" stamp in it from a Researcher down at the Oriental Institute at the University of Chicago, which makes me wonder how it ended up at the Book Fair (a lot of their books come from the estates of the recently deceased, and the previous owner, according to the Oriental Institute's web site, seems to be quite extant). Anyway ... if you don't know a lot about Mohenjo-Daro and Harappa, and find the subject of interest, you may want to track down a copy of this book!

Notes:

1. http://btripp-books.livejournal.com/80235.html
2-3. http://amzn.to/21P2ikf

Saturday, August 8, 2009[1]

What should I be when I grow up?

As those of you who are following along with my main journal know, I am presently, in the charming euphemism, "between jobs", and am spending the bulk of my time trying to find the "next opportunity" out there (lovely economy for it). So, I have been dusting off some job search books that I had lying around from my *last* time through the ranks of the painfully unemployed, and Carol Eikleberry's The Career Guide for Creative and Unconventional People[2] is one of these.

As one would deduce from the title, this is a book primarily aimed at "Artistic" folks, as defined by John Holland's theory of personality types. The first part of the book deals with finding one's "Holland code" and defining that. When I first picked up this a couple of years back, that's as far as I'd gotten, and used Eikleberry's rough estimation quiz to determine my code. This time I went off to the government's "O*Net"[3] site which offers all the "official" tools and took both the "Interest Profiler" and inter-related "Work Importance Locator". The former determines your scores in terms of the categories "Realistic", "Investigative", "Artistic", "Social", "Enterprising", and 'Conventional", while the latter ranks what you want to get out of work in terms of "Achievement", "Independence", "Recognition", "Working Conditions", "Relationships", and "Support". Eikleberry only deals with the former here, and, while from her quizzes I looked like an "AIR" (Artistic, Investigative, Realistic ... which pretty much leaves you with "Architect"), the O*Net tests put me pretty solidly as just an IA, scoring a 25/30 for "Investigative", 18/30 for "Artistic", with the next highest being just a 3 (and with 2 categories at *zero*). Now, lest one think that I was running off and getting "external feedback", the author encourages readers to use these services, and has many recommended on her http://creativecareers.com web site as well.

Once the reader has determined their "Holland Code", the book spends a while putting the "Artistic" personality into context, discussing how creativity can be expressed in various areas, discussing historical cases (such as Wallace Stevens and T.S. Elliot who both had "suit" jobs by day but produced significant literature in their free time), and the challenges and opportunities of having this sort of mind-set.

The middle section of the book deals with practicalities of searching out one's career path, from various general options ("run a small business", "teach in your field", etc.) to a whole collection of functional behaviors ("create a career notebook", "develop a relationship with a mentor", "resist perfectionism", "give yourself time", etc.)

The last third of the book is the weakest, however, as it's simply a long list of possible occupations, grouped into the authors' broad "Career Trails" of "Ideas", "Ideas and People", and "Ideas and Things", which are then subdivided into categories such as "Writers", "Negotiators", "Performers", "Finishers", etc. Each of the hundreds of individual careers briefly sketched out under these is given a 3-letter "Holland Code", but because the list is sorted from the "broad strokes" down, there's no way (short of going through each) to search out one's specific code matches (note: if one does the O*Net instruments, the results in their analysis tools are sorted by code, making it much easier to get a sense of "where one fits").

I was amused to find that nearly everything that I've ever done professionally, and most of the things that I had planned and/or considered doing, were right in my profile categories. Admittedly, this time around, my score being Investigative/Artistic/??? left things a bit open-ended, as the third factor was pretty much not a factor.

Overall, however, The Career Guide for Creative and Unconventional People[4] was a bit of a disappointment from my perspective. This could well be useful for somebody in *highschool*, wondering what to do with their life, or in college, trying to figure out a career that wouldn't "crush their soul", but there was little in here which spoke to me at my stage of life (unless I was suddenly able to "Get A Grant Or Find A Patron"), as I've already been down many of the roads suggested. I would certainly recommend that anybody picking this up follow the authors suggestions of using some of the other tools presented (such as the resources on the O*Net site), which gives a depth to the assessments not possible with just what's in these pages.

This 3rd Edition of the book is still in print, which will set you back $10-15.00 ... but previous versions are also available through the new/used vendors at Amazon, with "very good" copies going for as little as a penny and "new" copies at just shy of five bucks. Again, this is one of those books where "it depends" on where you are in life to how useful it would be to you. If you're looking at making a major change into an "Artistic" (or, generally "Creative") career path, there might be some very useful things in here for you, but if you've spent a quarter century doing stuff that's already in the book, not so much.

Notes:

1. http://btripp-books.livejournal.com/80558.html
2. http://amzn.to/24H0Wgx
3. http://www.onetcenter.org/
4. http://amzn.to/24H0Wgx

Sunday, August 9, 2009[1]
Peer amid?

This is another one of those "older books" ... another, in fact, that I picked up at the Newberry Library Book Fair a couple of weekends back. I note that it's "old" (and it's not all *that* old, having come out in 1974), because I recognize several things in here which are no longer the case due to research in the intervening 35 years, and I understand that there is also more stuff in here which is "dated" that I'm not familiar enough with to comment on.

That being said, The Riddle of the Pyramids[2] is a very interesting book. Written by a *physicist*, Kurt Mendelssohn (who had studied with Planck, Schrödinger, and Einstein in Germany and ended up in England after fleeing the Nazis), this spends 80% of its length looking at the pyramids of Egypt. The author claims to have somewhat "accidentally" come to writing the book, having made a connection between the dynamics of various landslides (in Wales) with the condition of "the collapsed pyramid" at Meidum. Fascinated by his perception (of the physics involved in the Meidum pyramid's collapse), he goes on to look at the entire period of pyramid construction.

The first half of the book pretty much looks at the construction of pyramids, from Mastabas, to the first "step" pyramids (which were essentially "stacking up" mastaba-type structures) to the evolution of the "true pyramid", and the eventual decline in pyramid building. The Meidum pyramid was built in three phases, a small step pyramid, a larger step pyramid, and eventually what would have been a "true" pyramid ... except that it (according to Mendelssohn) collapsed during construction of the third phase. The author looks at construction techniques, types of internal buttressing, the physics of materials under pressure, and then takes his conclusions from the specifics and expands to more general hypotheses.

One very interesting suggestion he makes is that the Egyptians did not actually know *pi*, even though the pyramids involve ratios that express that concept. He posits a "rolled cubit" measurement ... where *height* was determined by a linear measure (a hanging rope), but *length* was measured using a wheel with a diameter of a Royal Cubit, the tracing of the circumference creating a measure that inherently expressed *pi*, but all the Egyptian engineers needed to do was create ratios involving both measures. A 4:1 ratio resulted in the "true pyramid" angle of 51° 52', while a 3:1 ratio resulted in 43½°, the angle of the top of the "bent pyramid" and the "red pyramid"! Mendelssohn suggests that construction on the "bent" pyramid was well under way when Meidum collapsed, and that the angle was changed to the lower figure to avoid the same thing happening there. It was only when the ancient Egyptians figured out the *material* issues (those huge blocks of well-cut stone used at Giza), that they were able to successfully build the taller form.

The realization that there could well have been overlapping construction projects (Meidum and "bent") brings him to looking at the dynastic timelines, and finding that there are, during this particular period (as he was dating the construction by, there certainly is a lot of argument in this area that he simply side-steps), considerably more pyramids than Pharaohs to bury in them, and the construction projects seem to be on-going despite who was wearing the crown. This brings Mendelssohn to considering the *logistics* of building these monuments. Again, he side-steps the "technical" debate about how, specifically, the pyramids were made and (in true physicist fashion) simply breaks the problem down into how much "work" an individual human can do (in terms of, say, dragging a sled with a large stone on it), how much mass is involved in a given edifice, and figuring how many men over how many days it would take to get the blocks from the quarry and onto the pyramid (and then add on support, oversight, and technical staff estimated to be needed for that number of workers). He ends up with some charts which show how *difficult* it would be to "gear up" for one of these projects, but how reasonably easy it would be to *maintain* this on-going use of the population (for about 3 months a year, while the Nile was in flood and there was no agricultural work to be done), shifting resources between construction sites.

This then leads the author to another hypothesis. Looking at the uncertainty of the pyramids being specific burial sites, the on-going nature of the building process, he asks "what were they *for?*", and instead of coming up with some Sitchin-like scenario, he posits the pyramid building phase was a significant cultural shift, *creating* what we know today as "the state". Rather than having an unorganized web of small village structures, loosely controlled by a "divine" king who happened to have enough of an army to extract tribute and a certain degree of loyalty, there was now a *structure* which brought all these various minor entities into a common concern, over-seen by a organizational caste, working on a project that spanned many generations. He posits that the *end* of the "pyramid era" came when the tribal nature of Egyptian society had pretty much been erased by generations of "working for the state" on these huge construction projects ... once the *societal* goal was achieved, the "tool" for achieving that (building the pyramids) was no longer needed.

The book then takes a bit of a side-trip off to look at Mesoamerican pyramid building, and some general thoughts on how these sorts of huge "public works" projects become the defining elements of "the state". Ultimately he suggests that the "nation-state" which evolved from these various cultures (and has been humanity's primary organizational template for the past 5,000 years or so) has reached "in the nuclear era" (remember this was being written in 1974) a level of unsuitability that needs to be supplanted by a more global model, and asks what could be "our pyramids" that would erase the nation-state the way the Egyptians erased (or substantially supplanted) the village millennia ago. He suggests a unified space program which would focus vast resources over a long period of time on a project that might not have any true utility but could organizationally change the cultural template.

Anyway, The Riddle of the Pyramids[3] is out of print, so if you're interested in checking it out, you'll have to go through the used guys ... "very good" copies can be had for under a buck, and a couple of them have "new" copies for as little as $7.50 (plus shipping, of course). If you've read a lot of archaeology/Egyptology (as I have) this provides a thought-provoking "outside look" at the pyramid era which strips away all the religion (well, the book *does* deal with the issue, but more on an "organizational" level) and tries to specifically look at the function. Very interesting.

Notes:

1. http://btripp-books.livejournal.com/80888.html
2-3. http://amzn.to/21OZALs

Sunday, August 23, 2009[1]

Great book ...

This is another book that I got through LibraryThing's "Early Reviewer" program ... but it's the first time that I've gotten what is a classic "ARC" (advance review copy), which is for some reason amusing the heck out of me. Usually I've seen pretty much "bookstore ready" copies, but this is obviously an "in progress" project ... so I'm showing you what the book's *going* to look like and what the copy I got looks like here. There are various quirky things that I'm not used to seeing (all the page numbers on the Contents page are "000", waiting final edits!), but I guess we're not supposed to talk about those sorts of details.

Anyway, Mitch Horowitz' Occult America: The Secret History of How Mysticism Shaped Our Nation[2] is a *great* book. I've been very disappointed, generally speaking, with what I've seen from ER program over at LibraryThing (but, as the old saw goes: *whaddya want for nuthin'?*), and it's very pleasant to have a book come in from them that I'm extremely enthusiastic about. There's a particular type of book which serves as a jumping-off place for a whole spectrum of other reading, and this is one of those ... not only was it chock-full of information that I didn't *know*, in the course of reading it there were references to a good dozen *other* books that I'm now wanting to dig into.

The author here is a seasoned veteran of the publishing industry, and is widely known via articles and interview in the new age press, but this is his first book. I actually started reading this with the "about the author" and "acknowledgment" sections, and was wondering just how the book would read when he says *"An author stands on the shoulders of his editors."* before naming *four* editors that worked with him on this project (not counting the author himself!), and was pleased to find that this did not noticeably lead to a "written by committee" feel ... although there were a handful of "industry snarks" peppered in the text.

Occult America[3] is pretty much set up as a chronological account (although things do jump around a bit as it goes topic-to-topic), starting with some of the earliest settlers coming over to America in the 1690's and running up through Edgar Cayce. I was somewhat surprised that the book sort of "faded out" at the end, with not much of the '80s, '90s, or current decade's manifestations, but figured that the author was dealing more with "history" and some of the more recent organizations/movements are likely still "in flux" too much to add them to the things covered here. Frankly, the book is less about "the Occult" than it is something of a genealogy of the New Age movement. While Aleister Crowley gets *mentioned*, he's a peripheral figure (and I don't believe that, other than Regardie, any of his followers ... Parsons, etc. ... even get name-checked), I also don't recall Gurdjieff (or the "4th Way") making it into the book, or popularized

Sufism (outside of the fez-wearing crowd), and while there's a reference to Zen, the *actual* (as opposed to the Theosophical myth) Tibetan Vajrayana flowering here goes unnoticed. The focus of the book is very much on the "mainstream eccentric" (and generally Christian-based) traditions, from the Spiritualists in upstate New York to the likes of B.O.T.A. and AMORC and the various other "mail order" mystical traditions, weaving back and forth into Theosophy, Masonry, etc., often with political connections.

What is amazing is how long a lot of "The Laws of Attraction" / "The Secret" sort of stuff has been kicking around ... I've only recently delved into this particular end of the metaphysical universe, and was surprised to find that it's both been "done" to such a great extent and somewhat discouraged to find that its roots are less than esoteric (unless, of course, this material *did* appear via some "ascended master's" over-night crayon scribblings!) and more flim-flam than I would have preferred to think.

Again, I found this a riveting read, with bits and pieces of information that I wanted to rush right over to Amazon to check out, and I would certainly recommend it to anybody with an interest in "this sort of thing" (which I, needless to say, have). However, *as a reading experience*, the caveats above lead to a vague feeling of disappointment. While not asking it to be *encyclopedic* in its scope, it leaves out quite a lot in what seems to be an effort to focus on *individuals* (some having only transitory impact) who had influence in this area, and the "fading out" aspect makes it feel "unfinished" (unless, of course, the ARC that I was sent *is* prior to a final edit that would add material to give the narrative some closure). While I had been "generally aware" of several of the people/movements outlined in Occult America[4], the overall perception that this material "came out of the 60's" certainly gets eradicated and a far wider context is put in place, however, as noted, this does appear to be more a survey of the roots of the "New Age" movement than the "occult influences on America" that the title would suggest!

As this has not been officially released yet (the on-sale date is 9/15), I don't have any "money saving" suggestions other than that Amazon has pre-orders available at a 34% discount. I've already enthusiastically recommended this to several friends, and despite the points covered above, would encourage anybody interested in the subject to pick this up as a reference and jumping-off point for further research!

Notes:

1. http://btripp-books.livejournal.com/81115.html
2-4. http://amzn.to/21qyQ7K

Saturday, September 5, 2009[1]
Oddly disappointing ...

I've been familiar with Rupert Sheldrake's work for quite a while now, since having been introduced to his concepts of "morphic resonance" twenty years or so ago. I was really looking forward to reading his The Presence of the Past: Morphic Resonance and the Habits of Nature[2], expecting it to be filled with the sorts of gripping concepts that fill some of his other books. Unfortunately, this (for me, at least) did not seem to be the case.

Rather than charging off into new directions, the focus of this book seems to be trying to fit in "morphic resonance/ fields" within the context of evolutionary science, and, as such, spends most of its time framing elements of the latter, and then over-laying "morphic" elements to explain various particulars. Now, this is not to say that this isn't *fascinating* in places, but (again, for me) the book really dragged while waiting for "the good parts". Perhaps most interesting here was a look at how genetic sequencing should not have the data depth to be able to achieve what standard gene theory would have it do as far as replicating systems, and proposing a "field of habit" (much like Waddington's "Chreodes") that would guide development along established paths, something along the lines of how Roman carriages' wheel bases (by way of creating defined ruts in well-traveled roads) eventually determined railway gauges, which were a limiting factor in various parts of our space program.

If you're not familiar with Sheldrake's work, he's the "hundredth monkey" guy ... who suggested that once a novel behavior, achievement, or synthesis, has been actualized (in the case of the monkeys, it had to do with washing sand off of fruit, and when a sufficient number of monkeys in one region picked up this habit, it quickly spread to similar monkeys in geographically isolated areas), it becomes easier to repeat (another example is the synthesis of new forms of crystals in the lab, once a crystal has been successfully developed in one place, it becomes vastly easier to create elsewhere). Sheldrake popularized the concept of the "morphic field" which would carry the impression of these "forms" which would then be available to steer further similar situations towards similar ends. Of course, there is no hard evidence of how/where these fields might exist (and Sheldrake admits this), but he has reasonably convincing arguments that they have at least a fair likelihood of being there. For an example of "how this would work", think of the classic grade-school science experiment with a bar magnet, a sheet of paper, and iron filings. We can't *see* the lines of magnetic force from the magnet, until we sprinkle the filings on the paper above the magnet. Sheldrake would have it that Morphic Fields work similarly to drive behavior and evolution, even if we can't identify the "bar magnet" of their force.

Of course, Morphic Fields could go a long way to explaining the similar development of assorted marsupials related to the placental animals filling extremely similar niches elsewhere, as one example. Sheldrake also spends a lot of time looking at previous philosophical approaches to the issues at hand, and tries to fit in his theories within these contexts as well. Additionally, throughout the book he has suggested experiments that could be performed to test various aspects of the theory, as well as reporting on ones that could suggest its activity. One among these involved taking a well-loved Japanese nursery rhyme, along with two similarly-constructed rhymes, one that made sense, and one that was just random words. The one known to generations of Japanese children was best recalled by the mono-lingual American test subjects 62% half an hour after a session where all three were repeatedly recited (one would expect a 33% rate).

Anyway, I'm sure that other readers would likely find this of more interest than I did. It's got a lot of good stuff in it, but it's aim seems to be putting Sheldrake's theories into certain contexts, and in this effort a whole lot of (to me) less interesting stuff gets covered. The Presence of the Past[3] does appear to still be in print, so you should be able to find it at your local brick-and-mortar book vendor, but Amazon has it at a third off and their new/used vendors have "new" copies for just a few bucks. If you're a "life sciences" fan this would likely be a much better read for you than it was for me!

Notes:

1. http://btripp-books.livejournal.com/81252.html

2-3. http://amzn.to/1s5xZtJ

Sunday, September 6, 2009[1]

Some other place ...

I've been a fan of the Baigent/Leigh/Lincoln books for quite a while, although, as various spin-offs and other books have come out, it would appear that the *Priory of Zion* thing is either the world's most convoluted and well-hidden conspiracy or just smoke being blown to cover other, perhaps more mundane, conspiracies (see this[2]). After a couple of books, the "Holy Blood, Holy Grail" trio broke off into other groupings and projects, but Henry Lincoln (whose vacation read led to the all this verbiage, as noted in "The Holy Place") seems to have stayed relatively close to the subject. He also seems to be the main guy focused on tracing out geometric patterns over the landscape and obsessing on the math involved. We get more of this in The Templars' Secret Island: The Knights, The Priest, and The Treasure[3], a book co-authored with Danish documentary filmmaker Erling Haagensen, who *lives* on the title's island.

Most of this book is centered on the Danish island on Bornholm in the Baltic Sea, which appears to have had a long history as a "sacred space" (over a thousand megalithic standing stones are spread around this relatively small island, and these are fairly rare in Scandinavia), and there are fifteen stone churches that date from around 1200ce, including four unusual "round" churches. Lincoln and his associates here spend a great deal of effort trying to chart out relationships between these various constructions, ending up with some extremely complicated geometry.

Now, I'm willing to admit that maybe I just "don't get" the obsession on these lines, angles, and repeated geometries, but it seems to me that the more convoluted the form gets, the more likely it is that somebody is trying to find *some* line that goes through something! This especially comes to mind when there are convenient omissions of buildings (at least two of the Bornholm churches don't make it into these graphs), and equally convenient inclusions of otherwise unremarkable locations, made special only in being at some point of intersecting lines, or being the center point for some form, or being the apex of an angle (heck, point C/111 here is several miles offshore with no solid object to anchor it!). Again, this may simply be a personal failing on my part (I have had many friends over the years who found this sort of mathematical game *riveting*), with my inability to work up enthusiasm for these "revelations" arising from my relatively "untutored" state for this sort of number play. Or not.

I will admit (ceding the author the benefit of the doubt on his numbers/measurements, here benefiting by a detailed charting of the island by the Danish government) that some of the "precision" involved is quite striking, assuming that one accepts the base premise that structure one is on this circle, and that structure two is on that line that intersects with something else and that structure three is on a facing of another shape within that circle, etc. Needless to say, I'd be MUCH more impressed if these structures were laid out even in an equilateral triangle, or *square* on the island, to the level of precision of distance and angle that's being proposed here ... but including one structure on each corner point. *That* would be something that I could look at and "get"!

One would think, then, that this book would be a profoundly disappointing read when ("spoiler" alert!) one finds that the "treasure" of Bornholm *is this geometry/mathematics*. Yep, the old "encoding knowledge for the ages in stone" trick. Lincoln argues reasonably convincingly that this is what the whole 10th-12th Century Bornholm thing was about. However, what *saves* the book (for me, at least) is the bits and pieces of background information regarding the Templars, and the tradition of "Swedish Freemasonry". I was unaware that the Baltic countries such as Estonia had remained strongly Pagan and were "inconvenient" to the Holy Roman Empire as they formed a choke point to trade ... the Templars were called in to aid in a long battle with these tribes. Also, there are threads here that the Templars had a "special relationship" with Swedish/Scandinavian secret groups which resulted in a surviving undercurrent beyond the 1312ce dissolution of the order by Rome. Obviously, the Templars (whose "round" church design is evident here) were very involved in the region, and it is interesting to contemplate how that influence came (as has been rumored in many other books) to shape the Masonic orders. There are also some additional interesting bits regarding the Templar Knights in Jerusalem, and some of the events in Southern France, with the Merovingians, etc., and recent research showing so-far-unexplored "subterranean chambers" existing under many of the discussed structures. Oh, one "geometric" thing of interest here ... Bornholm and Rennes-le-Chateau are "exactly" the same distance from Jerusalem, at an angle which suggests the point of a pentagram.

Anyway ... the version I have of The Templars' Secret Island[4] is the Barnes & Nobel printing, which I got on clearance at the store (so I'm guessing it's out of print), but is still available on their web site. Deeply discounted copies can be found via Amazon's new/used vendors as well. Again, there is enough peripheral stuff in this book to make it well worth reading for somebody with as much of this material in one's library as I have, and I'm sure it would be *fascinating* to the "math game" inclined, and it's an interesting from a "Scandinavian history" level, but it just wasn't really "my cup of tea" (although I'm looking forward to further reading based on some of that "peripheral stuff"!) at this point ... however, as Dennis Miller would put it, "your mileage may vary"!

Notes:

1. http://btripp-books.livejournal.com/81479.html
2. http://btripp-books.livejournal.com/67093.html
3-4. http://amzn.to/1WhitXs

Friday, September 11, 2009[1]

Help for the job hunt ...

I have had the pleasure of making Conor Cunneen's acquaintance over the past few years, although I would have preferred the situations being different than my having been in repeated *job searches*. A few years back I'd reviewed[2] his *Why Ireland Never Invaded America*, and the current book, SHEIFGAB the World: 8 Building Blocks to Successful Job Transition[3] is something of a follow-up to that, featuring the same main character, the Irish business consultant Finbarr Kozlowski (the surname arising from his grandmother having "married a Scotsman" ... don't ask).

Finbarr claims that "SHEIFGAB" is an Irish word for "Do It" or "Make It Happen" (eventually admitting that it's only an Irish word in that it's a word made up by an Irishman), but it's actually the acronym created by the 8 "building blocks" of Cunneen's system:

>**S**tructure
>**H**elp
>**E**nvironment
>**I**mprove
>**F**amily
>**G**oals
>**A**ttitude
>**B**ehavior

Now, I have (unfortunately) been exposed to *many* job-search speakers over the past decade, and Conor Cunneen presents the most integrated system for dealing with this deeply unsettling life situation. Rather than approach the challenge of "being in transition" from a "details" approach (there's nothing here about how to research job leads, how to tweak your resume, etc.), SHEIFGAB is a "lifestyle" approach that addresses assorted aspects of the job-*seeker's* new situation.

The book is presented as a series of workshops that Finbarr is giving for a group of "NIGEPs" ... another acronym, this time for Non-Income Generating Employed Person, "banning" (as counter-productive) the term "unemployed", as when one is in the job search one is conducting the Most Important Job, so one is "employed" in that ... with each of the 8 topics being the subject of a session. One of the key messages, which resurfaces frequently through the book, is how *common* the transition experience is, and how many very successful people had significant "rough spots" on their way to the top. By using the scenario of a workshop with various attending members, Cunneen is able to reflect the assorted component messages off a spectrum of personality types, enabling most readers to identify with specific reactions. Obviously, he's given this presentation to enough groups that he's been able to sort out the most likely stumbling blocks and gives Finbarr approaches for countering these.

SHEIFGAB can really be broken into two parts, SHEIF, which is pretty much focused on the job seeker, and GAB which seems to be a more general approach that Cunneen also presents to other audiences. As one would guess from the list above, the system starts with *Structuring* one's approach to the job search. Keeping schedules, being on time for networking events, planning out one's time as though one were *working* at the Job Search, all these are elements without which it's hard to put any sort of organized effort together. Then there's *Help*, and this isn't just "reaching out" to friends and associates, it's also the job seeker *helping* others (volunteering, etc.), which provides emotional strength in trying times. Next there's *Environment*, which is pretty much the one part of the system where I fall down, as Finbarr/Conor suggests a nice tidy work space, and getting out of the house to bookstores, coffee houses, etc. to not "do the same thing in the same way at the same time in the same place" (I, personally, would have to drag a printer with me over to Barnes & Noble, so have not figured out a good way of working that; and my work spaces have always been chaotic!). This is followed by *Improve* ... this isn't simply the "go learn new skills" sort of advice, but a push for feeding in *positive* messages (taking out motivational tapes from the library, etc.) as well as working diligently to improve one's interviewing presence. Finally, in this section there's *Family*, which deals with the reality of having the usually out-of-the-house breadwinner *in* the house and, well, *not winning bread*. In this Cunneen presents an interesting concept, that of "taking others' parking spaces", where the job seeker might well be creating a great deal of stress by being around but "not doing anything" in the house (trash, shopping, cleaning, cooking, etc.), or by hogging time on a computer system that others might be used to having at their disposal.

The second part of this starts with *Goals*, which includes such obscure items as B-HAGs, S-HAGs, and NAGs. I'll leave the first couple of those to you to figure out (hint: the "G" is, not surprisingly, for "goals"), but will let you in on the NAG being a "Networking Accountability Group", which will, when established between one and some of one's NIGEP associates, *nag* one (in essence, taking the role of a Boss) if one isn't being accountable! This section also deals a lot with other networking strategies, some audacious, some just good ideas. Next there's *Attitude*, much of which plays off the example of Viktor Frankl, with methods to keep one's head in a productive space. This also parlays into a second "A", of ageism, which gets countered with a lot of Rock Star examples and a list of action points on how to make age relatively irrelevant, with a section on using Social Media (that new-fangled stuff all the kids are into) also tucked in here. Finally, there's *Behavior/Brand*, where one's behavior helps to establish one's brand (Cunneen's "brand promise" for his speaking biz is "E4 - Energize, Educate, Entertain & Easy to work with") and one's "brand" is what differentiates one in the eyes of potential employers.

Anyway, I highly recommend SHEIFGAB the World[4] to those in transition, or as a gift to present to those you know who are in transition. It's very reasonably priced, and if you order directly from Conor Cunneen's site, Irishman Speaks[5], he's got a special discount offer "to buy you a Guinness" (or maybe just pick up the shipping). It is available via Amazon as well, although I'm not sure about brick-and-mortar locations at this point (this is so "hot off the presses" that there's an anecdote about Michael Jackson's funeral in it!). Again, having this book is like having Cunneen and his SHEIF-GAB system at one's disposal for a week (or more) instead of just a couple of hours, so it is quite the value to anyone "between jobs"!

Notes:

1. http://btripp-books.livejournal.com/81778.html

2. http://btripp-books.livejournal.com/21716.html

3-4. http://amzn.to/24E2nMF

5. http://irishmanspeaks.com/store/publications/sheifgab-the-book/

Saturday, September 12, 2009[1]
Quite a treat ...

I was amazed to find that Faubion Bowers' The Classic Tradition of Haiku[2] was such a recent (1996) book. So many of the Dover Thrift Editions are re-prints of books long out of copyright, and I had assumed when ordering it that this would be some 19th Century exploration of this Japanese poetic style. I have a deep admiration and appreciation of Dover's commitment to producing this very inexpensive line of books, and am particularly so in the case of a book newly produced for the "Thrift" (the cover price of this being a mere $3) edition.

I was also not expecting much in terms of "instruction" from this volume, figuring that it would simply be a collection of assorted Haiku, perhaps with some basic chronological identifiers, but not much more than the translated poems. I was very pleased to find that Bowers' book goes far beyond that. The book is arranged chronologically, featuring 48 poets whose works span from 1488 to as late as 1902. Each has a brief biographical notation in a footnote, as well as years of birth and death. Every page (having 2-4 Haiku) features clarifying footnotes as well, putting various imagery and forms in context for the reader.

For those unfamiliar with the format of Haiku, it is typically a 3-line poem having 5, 7, and 5 syllables per line, although a variant has a 2-line coda following. One of the stylistic standards of the form is to have some connection with nature and some word involved that relates to the seasons (which is apparently a linguistic feature in Japanese much the way "gender" attributions make the Romance languages so confusing to native English speakers). Another attractive feature of this anthology is that each poem is presented in transliterated Japanese, so that one can get a sense of how they actually sound. In fact, most of the translators here have gone for "sense" rather than "format", so few (if any) of the English versions maintain the 5-7-5 structure.

Speaking of translators, the work of 45 experts is included here, ranging from the Editor's own contributions to those of Allen Ginsburg, with about 3/4 of the translations being culled from other works, and 1/4 apparently done specifically for this volume. Additionally, some of the more famous Haiku are presented with 2-3 versions by different hands.

Here are a few examples:

> Matsuo Bashō - (1644-1694)
> ***shirageshi ni / hane mogu chō no / katami kana***
> For the white poppy
> the butterfly breaks off its wing
> as a keepsake
>   *tr: Makoto Ueda*
> Mukai Kyorai - (1651-1704)
> ***hototogisu / naku ya hibari no / jūmonji***
> The cuckoo sings

> at right angles
> to the lark
> > tr: Burton Watson

> Kaga no Chiyo - (1703-1775)
> **wakakusa ya / kirema kirema ni / mizu no iro**
> green grass -
> between, between the blades
> the color of water
> > tr: Patricia Donegan & Yoshie Ishibashi

> Tagami Kikusha-ni - (1753-1826)
> **tama ni ge ni / mokutō ya tada / michi no tsuki**
> In spirit and in truth
> silent prayer ... just
> the moon on the road
> > tr: William J. Higginson

> Masaoka Shiki - (1867-1902)
> **ki o tsumite / yo no ake yasuki / komado kana**
> the tree cut,
> dawn breaks early
> at my little window
> > tr: Janine Beichman

Although brief, this little book is both beautiful and informative, from the editor's introductory essay through the multitudinous notes. I particularly enjoyed exercising my "menu Japanese" to read the poems out loud before reading the translations, as this gave at least a vague approximation of how these originally were meant to be.

This is in print, but (as is the case frequently with the Dover Thrift Editions) you are unlikely to find them at your local brick & mortar book vendor, as there's little room for a profitable mark-up. Once again, however, this is an ideal "throw in" for an Amazon order, to bump something up to the promised land of free shipping. Highly recommended!

Notes:

1. http://btripp-books.livejournal.com/82142.html
2. http://amzn.to/23zJ4OL1

Saturday, September 19, 2009[1]
Willing to try ...

I got this as a "throw-in" to get an Amazon order over $25 and into the free shipping zone ... little did I know how remarkable I'd find it. Originally written by Wallace D. Wattles in 1909, The New Science of Getting Rich[2] was one of the books that inspired Rhonda Byrne to develop *The Secret* and so spark the current "intention" industry. The version here (the dust jacket inserts a "new" in the title, although it doesn't appear anywhere else in the book) is from 2007 and is "edited" by Ruth L. Miller. I'm assuming (there is virtually no introductory or contextifying material aside from what's on the dust jacket) that this contribution was re-writing the book for the first section. You see, *this* version of The Science of Getting Rich features the text *twice* ... first in a "modernized" version, then in its original form.

Frankly, there isn't a whole lot of difference between the two ... reading the latter, original, version I expected to see a substantially different work, but this is hardly the case. Sure, "steel barons" and "plutocrats" are replaced with the likes of Fund Managers, etc., and some of the "technological" references (railroads, radio, etc.) are updated, but over-all the text is so similar that had the fact of one being updated with current cultural material not been pointed out, it could well have passed barely noticed. The most telling difference is that in the "new" version, each chapter has a summary specific to it ... which, I fear, was likely necessitated by the decline in educational preparedness in the century separating the two renditions! Of course, this does indicate that the book is rather short ... about 100 pages for each version ... but it also provides an impetus to re-read the text immediately, something that I, in my obsessive literary voraciousness, would be somewhat unlikely to do. However, this book might very well have caused me to re-read it (the author encourages one to *just* read this book until one's goals are attained), because it is rather extraordinary.

As regular followers of this space have no doubt observed, I have read a great deal of assorted metaphysical material from a wide array of traditions and sources, and have, over the past few years, added in quite a bit of the "intention/attraction" genre. As I read through this I was amazed to find close parallels to teachings originating in contexts as varied as Q'ero Shamanic practices, theories such as Sheldrake's "morphogenetic" fields, assorted cosmological models of advanced physics, and numerous pantheistic religious forms.

It could be argued that this *is* a "pantheistic" screed, as the core element to the underlying theory is that there is a "Formless Living Substance" which underlies and provides the material for the Universe, and that this substance is *intelligent* and manifests as "a great Living Presence, always moving inherently towards more life and fuller functioning". This is pretty much the only premise that one need accept to find the "science" of the book plausible, and even convincing (although there are some functional corollaries regarding formation of materials, such as *gold*, which I suspect need to be framed as coming from a more naïve scientific age).

Wattles walks the reader through various scenarios, and coaches for behaviors/mindsets which exhibit "a Certain Way" to approach things. In the original there is a "credo" built up section by section which is then repeated several times. To understand the book, this is key, so rather than discussing how he arrives at this, I'll simply present it here:

> *There is a thinking stuff from which all things are made and which, in its original state, permeates, penetrates, and fills the interspaces of the universe.*
>
> *A thought, in this substance, produces the thing that is imaged by the thought.*
>
> *Man can form things in his thought and, by impressing his thought upon formless substance, can cause the thing he thinks about to be created.*
>
> *In order to do this, man must pass from the competitive to the creative mind; he must form a clear mental picture of the things he wants and do, with faith and purpose, all that can be done each day, doing each separate thing in an efficient manner.*

And, of course, the Universe is constantly attempting to produce abundance, like vines covering every surface they can for further growth, so *being rich*, being able (to borrow an ad line from the U.S. Army) *to be all that you can be* (physically, intellectually, emotionally, spiritually) is the ultimate goal for the human being.

Needless to say, on its surface, this is hardly an onerous course of action in the pursuit of wealth, although the mental focus involved is quite a challenge. One has to reverse multitudinous "habitual patterns" of thought and behavior, always focusing on the idea that the Universe is busy manifesting the things that one wants. This dovetails well with Ekhart Tolle's "now" work, as following Tolle's approach it is easier to duck past some of the emotional stressors. It's also useful to keep in mind some of the *amazing* research that Lynn McTaggert has reported on which show the interplay of the mind and intention with real-world results.

Perhaps this synchs better with me than many of the other intention books because there are so many "threads" from my reading involved, but I am quite enthusiastic about The New Science of Getting Rich[3], and would recommend it to everybody. As noted above, I got this as a "throw-in" as, at the time when I ordered it, Amazon had this for a mere $4.60 per copy, but I was disappointed to find (when checking there today) that the price had jumped up to very near cover (disabusing me of plans of ordering several copies this evening to hand out to friends & family). The book is very reasonably priced, however ($11.95 cover), and the new/used guys have "new" copies priced (even with shipping) at less than half of that, and you may be able to find deals on this (it does appear to be a "cut out" at this point) in your local brick-and-mortar book vendor. Again, this is pretty much the *best* "intention" book that I've encountered, so suggest you grab a copy!

Notes:

1. http://btripp-books.livejournal.com/82230.html
2-3. http://amzn.to/1WhgMcx

Sunday, October 4, 2009[1]
Kallisti!

So ... a week or so back there was this book fair ... and Daughter #1 and I made it there for the last hour, they were pretty much picked over, but I found this little gem (the only one I got). Needless to say, I'd read on-line versions of Principia Discordia[2] before, but I'd never had an actual copy of the book. I see that there are numerous versions of this available out there, but this particular edition is the 1991 one from IllumiNet Press, which I believe contains the original graphics from the various handmade volumes generated by Kerry Thornley (aka *Omar Khayyam Ravenhurst*) back in the 1960's.

For those who don't immediately recognize it, the Principia Discordia is the "founding document" of the generally-credited-as-satirical religion of Dicordianism, which worships the Greek Goddess of Discord, Eris. This volume is 1/3rd very interesting introduction (which I'm not sure is in other editions) and 2/3rds the main document. According to the introduction, Thornley and Gregory Hill (aka *Malaclypse The Younger*, credited as author), "in 1958 or 1959 in a bowling alley in Friendly Hills or maybe Santa Fe Springs, California", had an experience with Eris, which resulted in Her taking up residence in Thornley's pineal gland, thus generating all this fascinating text.

The edition at hand is (once out of the introduction) quite graphic, in a "pasted-on-a-lamppost broadsheet by unstable persons" kind of way, with each of the "canonical" 75 pages numbered with a numbering stamp (as 00075, etc) and generally tarted up with assorted random rubberstamps and purloined clipart. The official title is "Principia Discordia, or How I Found Goddess and What I Did To Her When I Found Her – Wherein is Explained Absolutely Everything Worth Knowing About Absolutely Anything", this being "The Magnum Opiate" of Malaclypse the Younger. The text meanders through various conspiracies, cosmologies, psychologies, and assorted theories about, well, *absolutely anything*, spinning out a strange (if somewhat incoherent) web of all things Erisian. The most familiar element here may be the symbol, "The Sacred Chao" which is a Yin-Yang symbol on its side with Eris' golden apple (inscribed with "Kallisti") on one side and a pentagon (symbolizing order) on the other, expressing how order breeds chaos and out of chaos ... well, there are *theories*.

For something so *odd*, Discordianism has had quite an effect in the culture. It claims The Church of Sub-Genius (of Bob Dobbs fame) as a sister religion, with Discordianism providing credentials as a "Pope"[3] and Sub-Genius providing credentials as a "Tsar"[4], with other obvious similarities. Because the Bavarian Illuminati "are totally infiltrated" into the Discordian ranks, Thornley also claims the cult of Eris to have been the inspiration for Wilson & Shea's *Illuminatus Trilogy*, and subsequent memetic ripples through the cultural unconsciousness. Of course Discordianism had its own inspirations, such as the strange figure of Emperor Norton, whose exploits get a certain amount of attention in the book (perhaps as a figure of "Discordian governance"?), but it would be impolite to the Goddess to imply that all this material did not emanate from her specific beneficence.

As noted, this copy of the Principia Discordia[5] is a long-gone and out-of-print edition (although copies are available via Amazon's new/used vendors, some with ridiculously high price tags), but other, more recent, versions do seem to be available, although if you're looking for the 60's graphics, it appears that you're going to have to go with used. On-line versions (such as http://www.principiadiscordia.com) are similar, but most seem to have been re-set in computer faces (or to HTML text), and so have lost a good deal of the retro charm

Notes:

1. http://btripp-books.livejournal.com/82475.html
2. http://amzn.to/1Wh6yJk
3. http://hyperdiscordia.crywalt.com/popecard.html
4. http://www.gunsanddopeparty.net/tsar-card.html
5. http://amzn.to/1Wh6yJk

Sunday, October 4, 2009[1]
About "what is" ...

Epictetus
ENCHIRIDION

I am somewhat bemused that just a day or so back, a reader of my regular journal (from whence these book reviews ultimately emerge) suggested this volume as something that I should read. He was pointing me to an on-line version (that I had, frankly, downloaded and printed out a few months back, being that most books composed a couple of millennia ago are well out of copyright and these days "out there" for the taking), however I had picked up a copy of the Dover Thrift Editions printing of Epictetus' Enchiridion[2] in the meanwhile (I needed another $2.50 to get to Amazon's free shipping level, as usual for these books) ... but one has to figure that the confluence of these various factors may well indicate that this was something advisable to inject into my mental stream at this point!

Epictetus was a Stoic philosopher who was born in the first century C.E., a student of Musonius Rufus, and teacher to Arrianus, who was responsible for collecting together his master's lecture notes into the *Enchiridion*, or "Manual", as a distillation of Epictetus' teachings. For those not familiar with the Stoics, here's a bit from the book's introduction on this philosophy:

> *In the Stoic view, our capacity to be happy is completely dependent on ourselves – how we treat ourselves, how we relate to others, and how we react to events in general. Events are good or bad only in terms of our reaction to them. We must not try to predict or control what happens, but merely to accept events with equanimity.*

It would appear from the biographical info that survives about Epictetus that he certainly had a lot of opportunity to practice these approaches, having been born in Phrygia a cripple, he ended up as a youth a slave in Rome, but managed to become a freeman, and be apprenticed to a philosopher of note.

The format here is a large number of relatively small blocks of text, the largest being about a page in length, the smallest, a single line. The *Enchiridion* proper just takes up 52 of these, with the rest of the book being "fragments" which have footnotes pointing to the opinions of various scholars as to the authenticity or provenance of many of the other 178. This is not a particularly *hopeful* philosophy, but it is not morbid either. The focus is on "what is" and getting one's perspective in a place where that is sufficient. Here are a few samplings:

> *Of things some are in our power, and others are not. In our power are opinion, movement toward a thing, desire, aversion (turning from a thing); and in a word, whatever are our own acts: not in our power are the body, property, reputation, offices*

(magisterial power), and in a word, whatever are not our own acts. ... (E-I)

Seek not that the things which happen should happen as you wish; but wish the things which happen to be as they are, and you will have a tranquil flow of life. (E-VIII)

It is not poverty which produces sorrow, but desire; nor does wealth release from fear, but reason (the power of reasoning). If then you acquire the power of reasoning, you will neither desire wealth nor complain of poverty. (F-XXV)

It is better by assenting to truth to conquer opinion, than by assenting to opinion to be conquered by truth. (F-XXXVIII)

As noted, assorted versions of Epictetus' Enchiridion[3] are available on the web, but I'm not sure if this particular one (with the "fragments") is out there (the ones I looked at didn't have that). Of course, you can get the hard-copy version with both parts from Amazon for a whopping $2.50 ... a perfect add-on for those times when you're just a bit short of the $25 free-shipping level!

Notes:

1. http://btripp-books.livejournal.com/82827.html

2-3. http://amzn.to/24DLbH5

Sunday, October 11, 2009[1]

Loved it, but a buck was about right ...

I had a good "dollar store day" yesterday, picking up $102.75 worth of books for $5 ... one of which was this little gem. I was surprised that The Wife was unaware of who Kinky Friedman[2] is, as I had been at least peripherally (I've never been drawn to much exposure to country music) aware of him since the 70's. If you're similarly unfamiliar with Kinky, he's a long-time "satirical" country musician (*Kinky Friedman & the Texas Jewboys*), an author of a couple of dozen mystery novels and various volumes of social commentary, a columnist for *Texas Monthly*, and recently a (serious) candidate for the Governorship of Texas. He's close with Bill Clinton, George Bush and Jesse Ventura ... and is pretty much a legend in the right circles.

Anyway, Cowboy Logic: The Wit and Wisdom of Kinky Friedman (and Some of His Friends)[3] is a collection of brief aphorisms from the Cowboy perspective, collected over a number of years. Crediting thirty or so friends, from Willie Nelson to Don Imus (who also contributed the dust jacket photo of Friedman), and from "Captain Midnight" to the aforementioned Gov. Ventura, he is probably most indebted to the classic "cowboy humor" illustrations of Ace Reid, several dozen of which appear throughout the book. Only in a rare handful of cases does he identify what *bon mot* came from which source, but this is explained in this snippet from the introduction:

> *This book was fun to put together, ought to be fun to read, and hopefully, will be a financial pleasure. It may seem deceptively simple, but I consider it to be one of the greatest literary achievements of my career. This is because is represents a lifetime of stealing other people's lines. That being as it may, I am proud to point out that nothing in this book has been borrowed. Even I would not sink that low.*

Now, I'm not much of a laugh-out-loud kind of guy, but this collection had me guffawing and irritating the family by reading them various bits, so I did quite enjoy the half an hour or so it took me to swing through this. Which is my one caveat here: there's not much meat on these papery bones. Sure, Sufi teacher Idries Shah can get away with a 200-page book[4] that's got a 2-page introduction and all otherwise blank pages (for $25) as a "teaching exercise", and avant-garde artist John Cage can be celebrated for 4'33"[5] ... but somehow the $17.95 cover price of this seems pretty steep for what is *certainly* under an hour of reading (albeit highly amusing reading). There are only *one* or *two* observations like the following on each page, padded out with the previously noted "cowboy cartoons":

> *Courtesy is owed. Respect is earned. Love is given.*
> -
> *A happy childhood is the worst possible preparation for life.*

> *I believe musicians can run this state better than politicians.*
> *We just won't get a lot done in the mornings.*
>
> *A lot of folks died in the Bible,*
> *but a hell of a lot more died because of it.*
>
> *Man's ability to delude himself is infinite.*
>
> *If you hear a Texan exclaim, "Hey, y'all, watch this!",*
> *stay out of his way. These are likely the last words he will every say.*
>
> *The art of writing fiction*
> *is to sail as dangerously close to the truth as possible*
> *without sinking the ship.*
>
> *Talent is its own reward.*
> *If you have it, don't expect anything else.*
>
> *One good aspect of being mediocre*
> *is that you're always at the top of your game.*

Again, this is not to say I didn't very much *enjoy* the book ... it's just that I suspect that it got into the "dollar store market" because it's a GREAT read for a buck, but would be an inner struggle (unless one was personally interested in supporting Friedman's political campaigns) at cover price.

If you can't find Cowboy Logic[6] at your local dollar emporium (it does seem to have been dumped into the aftermarket, appearing to be officially out-of-print after just over 3 years since its release), it can be had via the Amazon new/used guys for as little as 37¢ used or under $3 new (with, of course, the $3.99 shipping charge added on). I'd say if you stumble over this "out there" for cheap, do pick it up, as it's a fun read, but take into consideration that it's a *brief* read if your paying much more than I did!

Notes:

1. http://btripp-books.livejournal.com/83076.html
2. http://en.wikipedia.org/wiki/Kinky_Friedman
3. http://amzn.to/23zw0Je
4. http://amzn.to/2a928P3
5. https://goo.gl/tUc6SU
6. http://amzn.to/23zw0Je

Sunday, October 11, 2009[1]
A mixed bag ...

Pretty much every year we go to the Newberry Library Book Fair, a neighborhood tradition (nice to have the Newberry in the neighborhood!) that's been running for 25 years now. Recently, we've been just doing Sunday, which is the half-price day, and by then they're pretty picked over. I do seem to get some good finds ... this year including Beyond Ego: Transpersonal Dimensions in Psychology[2], a wide-ranging anthology edited by Roger N. Walsh, M.D., Ph.D, and Frances Vaughan, Ph.D.

I probably picked this up on the strength of the list of 16 contributors noted on the back cover, several of which, Fritjof Capra, Ken Wilber, Stanislav Grof, Charles Tart, Abraham Maslow, Ram Dass, and Jack Kornfield, I was reasonably familiar with. The book is, however, sort of one of those that tries to be two things at once, it is in parts very academic, while in others fairly "popular", swinging between extremes in the nature of the sections. The cause of this is in the fairly wide reach of the book, which looks at everything from traditional psychology to Eastern meditation practices, and from LSD research into how the "transpersonal" could come to effect fields such as Education and Social Sciences. It's divided into six main sections, "Wider Vision: New Paradigms For Old", "The Nature of Consciousness", "Psychological Well-Being: East and West", "Meditation: Doorway to the Transpersonal", "Transpersonal Psychotherapy", and "Ripples of Change: Implications for Other Disciplines", with 2-8 papers contributing to the discussion in each.

It would appear that, except for the editors' own contributions, the majority of the other pieces were reprinted or excerpted from previous publications. There were some interesting notes, however, which referred to papers within the volume, but that might simply be an editorial decision to point to the material at hand rather than to its source. Needless to say, an accumulation of diverse voices in widely divergent contexts leads to a highly uneven tone, and the "reading experience" was likewise a bit of a rollercoaster, shifting between analytical and experiential tones.

Over-all, this collection is "interesting", but I suspect that it will be more or less interesting depending on what the reader brings to the table. Here are a couple of samples from the book which illustrate how variable the text gets:

> Simple forgetting and lack of threshold response constitutes the subliminal submergent-unconscious. Dynamic or forceful forgetting, however, is repression proper, Freud's great discovery. The repressed submergent-unconscious is that aspect of the ground-unconscious which, upon emerging and picking up the surface structures, is then forcefully repressed or returned to uncon-

> *sciousness due to an incompatibility with conscious structures.*
>
> \- - -
>
> *The path to freedom is through detachment from your old habits of ego. Slowly you will arrive at a new and more profound integration of your experiences in a more evolved structure of the universe. That is, you will flow beyond the boundaries of your ego until ultimately you merge into the universe. At that point you have gone beyond ego. Until then you must break through old structures, develop broader structures, break through those, and develop still broader structures.*

While the over-all book is fascinating, it's not exactly a great read. There is a whole lot of information and perspective in here, so is valuable as something (to echo Truman Capote on writing) "to have read", but it's unlikely to show up on anybody's top-10 favorite books! Beyond Ego[3] is out of print (it came out in 1980) but is still available used. The Amazon guys have it for as little as 14¢ for a "good" copy, and under five bucks for "like new" (with, of course, the $3.99 shipping charge on top of that). If this is something that is in your "intellectual sweet spot", I'd certainly recommend it ... but if various sorts of psychology (traditional, Eastern, meditative, LSD, etc.) doesn't do much for you, I'd say skip it without much regrets. Again, it's got fascinating material in it, but it's a bit of a slog in parts.

Notes:

1. http://btripp-books.livejournal.com/83278.html
2-3. http://amzn.to/1rBoOjS

Friday, October 16, 2009[1]
Archaeological evidence of ...?

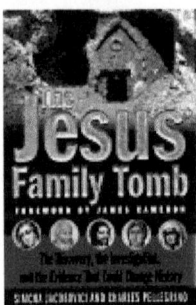

This was another dollar store find from a while back. I'd previously read James Tabor's The Jesus Dynasty, and initially thought that this was directly connected to that, but while Tabor's work is referred to here (and both books do appear to be based on the same archaeological discoveries), The Jesus Family Tomb: The Discovery, the Investigation, and the Evidence That Could Change History[2] is off in its own area. This is probably the third book that I've picked up at the dollar store that was the story of putting together a documentary ... must be some sort of trend ... and the authors of this, Simcha Jacobovici and Charles Pellegrino, have been involved in many documentaries and other film projects (including Titanic, which led to James Cameron doing the Foreword).

For those not familiar with the back-story, in 1980 a tomb was uncovered in the suburbs of Jerusalem in a construction project. This dated to the first century CE, a brief period in time when the "fashion" was using rock-cut tombs for temporary burial, followed by collecting the deceased's bones into an "ossuary" box. The "ossuary age" lasted not much more than a century, not coming into acceptable practice until just prior to New Testament times, and being wiped out (along with Jerusalem) in 70CE. In this "family tomb" there were several ossuaries, with names inscribed on them which matched names in "Jesus' family" including his own.

Now, long-time readers of this space will recall that I am a bit of an "anti-theist" and have serious doubts of the veracity of anything Biblical, but this could possibly be the *first* actual real-live *archaeological* evidence that the Jesus of the Bible was a historical figure and not just some (ala Allegro) meta-myth. The crux, if you will, of the argument here is in a statistical analysis of the names found in this tomb, along with some DNA analysis. Now, I don't want to give away all the details, but the tomb had appeared to have been sealed for a very long time, and had filled up with a silt that had preserved bits of organic matter. Some very interesting tests were done on these. The main "identifying factor", though, was in the matrix of names.

The book goes into a lot of "guesstimating" here ... the population of Jerusalem at that time, the frequency of the various names in the population, and the juxtaposition of the names as found in the tomb ... put through various mathematical contortions to determine the probability that these particular names would be found in this grouping at that time and not be "the holy family". The final count is something like 600 to 1 that this is, indeed the "family tomb" of *those people*, including the famed Jesus. Interestingly, one of the ossuaries was inscribed with the name of a Mary who had an additional name, not "Magdalene", but an earlier version "Mariamne" used to note *that* Mary which shows up in the apocrypha's Acts of Philip. One ossuary, which was charted *in situ* when the archaeologists opened the tomb, managed to disappear between the site and the museum ... and it would appear that this was the "James Ossuary" which found its way into a somewhat shady collector's hands near the same time. They note that had this name been added to the others, the odds would have improved markedly.

One of the most interesting parts of this whole story is how much this stuff just "swept under the rug" ... needless to say, there are those for whom the bones of a historical Jesus would be a major spanner in the whole "God" thing on the Christian side ... and from the Israeli side of things the whole Judeo-Christian period (the pre-Pauline Christianity, "Church of James" or Ebionites) seems to be an inconvenience. There is even evidence that a Franciscan monk had found (at a site called Dominus Flevit) the ossuary of St. Peter, an embarrassment to the Catholics who have spent centuries digging under the Vatican to find his tomb! None of these groups are particularly enthused about connecting the dots presented by the archaeological evidence, and would just as well have it fade to obscurity.

Despite The Jesus Family Tomb[3] being a "dollar store find" for me, it appears to be still available, at least via Amazon ... however, their new/used guys have "very good" copies for as little as a penny, with "like new" coming in at about 40¢ (plus the $3.99 shipping, of course). I would heartily recommend this book to most, with the one slight caveat that I have some questions about the math (more that I don't quite understand it, rather than I don't "buy it"), and much of the argument that this is what it appears to be hangs on those probability numbers. Again, this is the most convincing archaeology that I've seen pointing to the historical reality of *that guy*, so even "thumpers" should find this of interest!

Notes:

1. http://btripp-books.livejournal.com/83600.html

2-3. http://amzn.to/23zuO8L

Saturday, October 17, 2009[1]

What to say ...

Books like this remind me that there still is a role for *publishers* in the world of anyone-can-make-one print-on-demand book services. Back when I was running Eschaton Books, I had a few manuscripts come in "typeset" like this (or, actually, much worse, at least this isn't in a dozen different display faces!), with authors attached who were incredulous that you didn't think it looked *wonderful* (think "MySpace" vs. "LinkedIn").

Anyway, there's a story here. Last week I was giving a presentation to an agency on Second Life, which I'd been up working on for nearly 3 days straight, and following this, I figured I'd give myself some "me time" in a Starbucks in the neighborhood. I was reading the previously-reviewed book, and this odd fellow came by and seemed to want to talk about it. This was Dr. Richard Talsky, who is a guy with a lot of *plans* and a *modus operandi* which seems to focus on cornering the unsuspecting in the assorted coffee houses in which he holds court. Now, being that I'm "between jobs" and many of his "plans" involve the sort of skill sets that I am currently not using, I thought "oh, great!" and ended up getting sucked into spending a vast lot of time sitting in assorted Starbucks over the next couple of days (and setting up a whole array of Social Media sites for him). Unfortunately it appears that his main source of income at the moment is selling copies of 50 Ways to Thrive, Putting the Sizzle Back Into Your Life: A New Look at the Possibilities for Human Beings[2] to coffee shop customers, and most of the other plans seem to hinge on finding the right people who can make them magically appear (in full disclosure, I'm very likely going to be re-doing the layout of this book for him, whether he opts to use it or not). I'm still holding out a *slight* hope that he is able to move forward on some of these, as they could provide quite an interesting source of possible income for me it they did attain some degree of reality (see his site[3] for some details).

As one would guess ... this is a collection of various "methods" and/or approaches to "thriving", some based in familiar newagey territory, some running off into a world primarily occupied by Dr. Talsky. Content-wise (as opposed to the lay-out) it's no worse than many similar books out there, and it certainly looks at some different aspects that are not typically followed. I think it would be *greatly* improved by re-structuring, as in its current format it doesn't track particularly well, but the content, put in a more accessible form, might be worth what he's asking for it.

Anyway, I've noticed this new concept of "thriving" popping up in various contexts, so Dr. Talsky may be onto something here. His background started in art and advertising before becoming a chiropractor and practicing that for a quarter century. Again, many of his stories beg to be taken with many grains of salt, but he insists that he achieved rather remarkable results applying various of these insights to his business.

Although set up as 50 discreet elements, most of them function as part of a whole, so I'm not going to even try *listing* them here (they are, however, listed here[4]) ... while some are "common sense" or familiar "attraction/intent" modalities, they seem to work better as a whole than extracted. The current book is brief (under 100 pages) and claustrophobic (the edit I'm going to give it will expand that out a good deal), and has a rather steep $15.00 cover price ... although I got *mine* "in trade" for buying him a sandwich.

Now, you don't have to start haunting the various Starbucks on the near north side of Chicago to get a copy, the current version was published through Amazon's service, so is available on-line through them[5]. Although one of the "plans" is to get this out into a much wider distribution, I don't believe that it's either *in* any bookstores, nor available *through* them at the moment ... although you can also get an earlier version through LuLu. It's an interesting book, but certainly not everybody's "cup of tea".

Notes:

1. http://btripp-books.livejournal.com/83936.html
2. http://amzn.to/24DHX6v
3. http://thewowcenter.com/
4. http://thewowcenter.com/50ways/50_titles.html
5. http://amzn.to/24DHX6v

Saturday, October 24, 2009[1]

Pentagrams and Golden Sections again ...

I know what regular readers of this space are going to say: *"Brendan, why do you keep reading those books if you never really 'get' them?"* Point taken. Of course, I'm a sucker for a "good deal" and I found Nicholas R. Mann's The Sacred Geometry of Washington D.C.: The Integrity And Power of the Original Design[2] on a 75%-off clearance table at B&N a couple of months ago, and it looked *interesting*, was only two bucks, and so I picked it up.

Frankly, I was expecting this to be far more "woo-woo" that it was, following in the footsteps of the Dan Brown fellow-travelers (like several titles that have appeared here previously). On one hand, I was relieved to find that this was not really the case, however, on the other, when the author starts doing Henry Lincoln style "sacred geometry" tracing of complex patterns over maps, it really does help having some mystery, conspiracy, or Big Secrets to entice the reader to play along.

In this case, Mann runs the narrative closer to a history, with side-trips into philosophy (and not in the "mystery" zone), focusing on Major Pierre Charles L'Enfant, the French associate of George Washington who had been tasked with designing the new capitol city. There *is* a recurring question as to whether the Masons were involved (or, I suppose, *to what extent* Masonic philosophy was involved, being that Washington and many of the other leading lights of the day were very visible high-ranking Masons), but it's not *about* that.

The book looks at various influences "in play" at the time, from myths and legends current regarding the Native American tribes that had been in the area, to the emerging mythos of the U.S., and old-form European traditions. L'Enfant was from French aristocracy, his family being artists associated with the royal house (he'd even grown up at Versailles, the design of which seemed to have a not-inconsequential effect on his plans for DC), providing him with both a solid knowledge of European artistic and architectural systems, but also a less-than-democratic attitude (he seemed to regard Washington as his "royal patron") which eventually ran him afoul of Jefferson and other elements in the social weave of the day.

The downside of not having much of "a mystery" involved is that the book is, frankly, more *boring* than something that's purporting to lead up to a "big secret" (as disappointing as some of those sorts of books may end up). The author spends a substantial part of the text trying to re-create the "plan" that laid behind the eventual lay-out of Washington DC, talking about "golden section" relationships, "vesica piscis" orientations, *phi*s, *pi*s, and lots and lots of pentagrams (and a good part of it trying to explain why things didn't lay out "exactly" to these geometries). As I've noted before, I'd be *far* more impressed in one of these situations if five substantial geographic locations (buildings, monuments, squares, etc.) *precisely* showed up on the five points of a pentagram, but somehow it's always 3-4 points "suggesting" an alignment, but no solid proof for the entire form. Admittedly, the alignments in DC *do* appear to be very clearly aligned to these sorts of geometries, but the whole still suffers from "woulda coulda shoulda" *assumptions* of "intent".

One thing I found somewhat surprising (and, obviously, not in a *good way*) was how many blatant typos found their way onto the printed page here ... there were *several* instances where a "1790's" date was rendered a "1970's" date (!) and other places where subordinate clauses were pointlessly repeated (indicating a cut-and-paste that hadn't been cleaned up). Having been an editor and a publisher, this sort of thing makes me wonder how much attention was given this project!

SPOILER ALERT! (for those folks on LibraryThing.com who are always whining about reviews that "spoil" the read) ... in the final analysis, Mann feels that L'Enfant's design was very much his own creation, based on his background in the arts and architecture of Europe, and the mathematics that are implicit in the design of the city are more "classical" than the "mystical" systems that would have likely been expressed had the plan been "Masonic" (he contrasts this with the Washington Monument, which has geometries of a far more Masonic sort).

Again The Sacred Geometry of Washington D.C.[3] is an *interesting* book, and can be appreciated as a history of the efforts of a notable contributor towards the definition of the USA, but almost *hampered* by the whole "let's draw *pentagrams* on the map!" aspects. Despite my getting this on "clearance", it's still available from bn.com ... although (as is often the case for B&N published books) only available in the "aftermarket" via Amazon. If you find this sort of geometric symbology *fascinating*, by all means pick this up; if you're interested in post-revolutionary history, you'll likely find this reasonably engaging; but if you're looking for Deep Dark Secrets worthy of a Nicolas Cage adventure, I think you'll be disappointed in this book ... as always, YMMV, but with a cover price of $7.95 for a hardcover, you won't be out much getting it.

Notes:

1. http://btripp-books.livejournal.com/84056.html

2-3. http://amzn.to/1kWirEq

Wednesday, October 28, 2009[1]

Well ...

As anyone who regularly follows this space will tell you, I don't have exactly "popular" reading habits, and somewhere around *half* the time over on LibraryThing[2], I'll be the only person reviewing a particular book, and one of only a handful having a copy. Needless to say, in the case of Steven D. Levitt & Stephen J. Dubner's Freakonomics: A Rogue Economist Explores the Hidden Side of Everything[3], this is not the case (with over 12,000 copies logged in there, it's the 70th "most popular book", and it's been reviewed nearly 250 times). While this doesn't "cross the line" over into Fiction (for the past several years I have read only non-fiction), it has that "well, what do you *say* about a book that so many people have already read?" vibe about it, which I find oddly unsettling when looking at doing a review. On top of that, a follow-up edition ("Superfreakonomics"[4] ... insert your own Rick James reference here) just came out, so there's buzz about on the subject, making my adding to the verbiage seem somewhat superfluous.

I ended up reading Freakonomics by a bit more direct route than is typical of my recent acquisitions ... at the open session of this summer's Ad:Tech conference here in Chicago, the noted "chief innovation officer" for the Publicis Group, Rishad Tobaccowala, *strongly* recommended that if one hadn't read the book, one should make a point of doing so. In my recent job search, I have become quite "coachable" when it comes to suggestions from the leading lights in the fields where I'd like to be working, so I promptly put in an order with Amazon for a copy.

For those of you *not* familiar with the book, it is a collaboration of a noted economist, Levitt, and a former NY Times editor, Dubner. The book arose from Levitt's application of economic theory to various societal issues, with frequently unsettling results (the "central idea" of the book is rendered: *"if morality represents how people would like to world to work, then economics shows how it actually does work"*). This starts out fairly straight-forwardly, with an analysis that helped filter out "cheating" teachers in the Chicago Public School system, and then mirroring this with a look at how Japanese Sumo wrestling appears to be "fixed". The book would have been a much dryer read, however, if it had stayed in a strictly numerical zone like that, but it soon shifts into a more general range, looking at how the Ku Klux Klan was battled by opponents who focused on airing its secrets, and how, without the aura of those secrets, the organization lost much of its appeal, and comparing this with the reality of *real estate agents* using their "secrets" to frequently make deals that are not in the full interest of their clients.

The middle sections of the book are the most controversial, first looking at inner-city drug dealing as a business, which the authors end up considering not much different, structurally, than a fast-food chain, or other highly stratified corporate entity, as a way of answering the question "why do drug dealers still live with their moms?" (short answer: the average gang member typically clears less than minimum wage while the "obscene profits" concentrate at the top of the organization). Most notable, of course, is the section on why, contrary to all forecasts in the 80's and 90's, did crime suddenly *drop*. The analysis here points not to "new policing strategies", not to the economic boom of the era, but to the effects of Roe vs. Wade ... that substantial chunks of what would have been a whole generation of criminals were *aborted* in the inner cities, and rather than "coming of age" as a predicted wave of street thugs, appeared as a major gap in the numbers. Needless to say, this was a horrific concept to both the Religious Right and the Lenient Left, and gave the authors their biggest notoriety.

The last sections deal primarily with parenting, with many "counter-intuitive" revelations about what is and what isn't important in raising kids, at least as the numbers indicate. I must admit that I had some firmly-held opinions challenged here regarding the value of certain things we worked hard to put in place for *our* kids. This then moves back into controversial areas with a look at naming patterns, and how black kids end up with names which are likely to stigmatize them (in terms of moving into mainstream society), as well as to long-term patterns of name use.

What I believe that Mr. Tobaccowala was getting at in so strongly recommending this book is to be in a place where one questions "the conventional wisdom" and looks beyond the surface appearances of societal features. Certainly (despite "the numbers" presented here), much in Freakonomics[5] can be taken with a grain of salt, but it is something of a light being shone into areas not specifically considered previously.

As one might expect, this is widely available, and would no doubt be in stock at your local brick-and-mortar book vendor; however, Amazon has it at almost half (42% discount) off of cover, which is quite a deal (and on a par with the available used copies), so that's likely your best bet, if this is something that you've "been meaning to get around to reading".

Notes:

1. http://btripp-books.livejournal.com/84471.html
2. http://btripp-books.com/
3. http://amzn.to/1ImesvB
4. http://btripp-books.livejournal.com/89019.html
5. http://amzn.to/1ImesvB

Wednesday, October 28, 2009[1]

Quite a good read ...

This is another "dollar store find" that falls into the "*how did that get there?*" category ... it's scarcely three years old, and is quite an engaging read, yet it's already "remaindered". My best guess is that Timothy Dobbins' Stepping Up: Make Decisions that Matter[2] "fell between the cracks", category-wise, as it was published by the "business" side of Harper-Collins, but it reads much more like a "self-development" book. If this was being marketed to the "business management" sector, I can see why it might have failed to the extent that they'd drop it, which is unfortunate, as this is quite a perceptive and useful book ... too bad they didn't "change gears" and point it at the "newage" market!

The author is an interesting figure in that he started out as an Episcopalian priest (which he still is, on the side) who evolved into a business coach/consultant. These roots are notable throughout, as much of his approach has the "pastoral counseling" vibe, although generally dealing with business-centered situations. He begins the book with a look at how people search for meaning in the face of emptiness, which is a very worthwhile essay in its own right. I especially appreciated how he clarified the roles of spirituality and religion:

> Spirituality is about the human spirit and soul; how each of us individually and collectively become conscious of ourselves and our unique roles in the universe. It's an expression of our values and beliefs. Religion, on the other hand, is a particular system of faith and belief with its own set of rules and practices.

... this in a discussion of how *spirituality* "belongs not only in places of worship, but in the workplace ... (being) central to our full humanity". This is a well focused point, and one that is egregiously lacking in our culture as a whole (although there are far too many people desiring to bring their *religious* biases into the workplace). His concept of "stepping up" is doing the "right thing" as far as our personal (spiritual) authenticity is concerned, and the book is an examination of why, most of the time, people opt for other strategies.

Dobbins defines these other strategies as: "Standing Still", "Stepping Aside", "Stepping Back", and "Stepping on Someone Else", each getting its own chapter filled with stories of people he's encountered and how they manifested these, contrasted with those who actually "stepped up". Here are the "thumbnail" definitions for these:

> **Standing Still:** Standing still is the default option for almost all of us. To stand still is to let something happen without taking any action. Things might work out, or they might not, but in either case your action is inaction.
>
> **Stepping Aside:** If standing still is ignoring your responsibility, stepping aside can be an abdication. It's

> taking yourself out of the game, giving up, waving a white flag, and telling someone else to take your place.
>
> **Stepping Back:** *We step back to block others from moving forward. Often workplace stepping back takes place in team or group projects. Consciously or unconsciously you block the team or group from moving in a direction that may not meet your own needs.*
>
> **Stepping on Someone Else:** *Business is almost always portrayed as a zero-sum game ... (but) I don't believe it's true of most of the interactions between individuals ... just because your company's goal is to take market share away from your competitors, that doesn't mean your personal goal needs to be to take responsibilities and power away from your coworkers.*
>
> And, finally, **Stepping Up:** *.. (W)e almost always know what the right thing to do is in any given situation ... the answer is almost always there, somewhere inside ... in most situations we have a general sense of what should be done, or what needs to be done ... if you give yourself a chance, you'll know what you need to do to step up.*

The author takes on each of these, with examples both from his own immediate surroundings (and actions), and those more "generally" presented (although he does indicate that the stories all represent actual situations). While nothing here is particularly "earth shattering", it does give plenty of places to consider one's own behavior, and how to manage these various "strategies" when they are manifesting around one in the work environment (and, of course, elsewhere).

Again, I was happy to have encountered Stepping Up[3], and would recommend it to anybody. The tone, for me, was "just right" between not being "preachy" and not being "consultant-y", and the structure of the information made for very effective delivery. As noted, this seems to be only available in the "aftermarket", so if you can't find it at your local dollar store, you can snag copies from the Amazon new/used vendors of "like new" books for as little as 1¢ (plus, of course, the $3.99 shipping). It's a very useful little volume, and I do hope the author manages to find a new publisher for it, as it really doesn't deserve its present fate!

Notes:

1. http://btripp-books.livejournal.com/84508.html

2-3. http://amzn.to/24DGihk

Sunday, November 8, 2009[1]

Would be nice ...

A few weeks back I'd attended a Social Media Club "MeetUp" that featured Mark Victor Hansen and Robert G. Allen. I was pretty excited about this, as these guys are "keynote" caliber speakers, and it was cool to have them in a much smaller room. It soon became clear that the *reason* that we had them available was that the were out on a whirlwind tour flogging their new book (and offering a heck of a deal on "extra stuff" if you bought a copy that night). Well, when I started looking into the new book's info, it became clear that it was sort of a "Volume 2" to their previous book The One Minute Millionaire: The Enlightened Way to Wealth[2], so I figured it would make sense for me to get this (via Amazon's used vendors, of course) and read it first.

Now, as regular readers of this space will no doubt recall, I have been out of work for quite a long time, and have been trying to find *something* that will bring in money. As such, I was well-primed for Hansen & Allen's spiel. However, I think a couple of caveats need to be put forth from the start. This book came out in 2002. The economy in 2002 was apples-to-oranges to the economy of 2009. I, frankly, believe that a *lot* of what was "sage advice" in 2002 is more of a "recipe for disaster" in 2009, especially in their favored Real Estate pathway ... this is likely why they've come out with the new book! This is, of course, not to say that the book is *worthless* at this point, I'm sure that the general structure and approach they detail is still quite valid, only that the specifics have changed with the economic times.

The other caveat I have is that this book (and its follow-up) are *strangely* formatted, which has the potential to derail the information flow. The right hand pages are a "novella" about a young lady encountering a millionaire "master mind" group, becoming the protégé of one of these, and forming her own group to achieve a very difficult task (I will leave the details out for those of you who loathe "spoilers") in a very short period of time ... specifically, needing to come up with a million dollars of cash within three months (starting with *nothing*). The left hand pages are the "manual", as it were, which gives the reader the basic course in the Hansen/Allen "system". The authors suggest approaching this however you want, reading one first and then the other, or working through them in tandem. I opted for the latter approach, which ended up with a lot of "jumping around" as sections of the story rarely ended on pages facing sections of the manual! Also, the story has (every now and again) what look like foot/endnote superscipts which refer to pages in the manual ... however, this seems to be a bit haphazard, at least in terms of how I went through the book. Back in my publishing days, I did a book that was half&half like this, combining a thriller novella with an NLP training manual, but in that case we did the fiction first and had the manual being essentially a lengthy appendix on how the protagonist had been trained. In the case of The One Minute Millionaire[3] I think the most *effective* approach would be to read the *manual* first to get a grounding in the concepts, then read through the *story*, at which point the various back-references to the manual would make more sense!

Hansen and Allen had set themselves a "goal" of creating a million "Enlightened Millionaires" with their books, courses, seminars, etc., and there is a smattering of their "philosophy" behind this. Again, rather than just put it out here (that would sort of be a "non-fiction spoiler", wouldn't it), I'll just say that it puts the rest of the stuff into a context that keeps bits and pieces that might be seen, on their own, as "heading off into left field" corralled into a largely coherent approach.

The section headings for the "manual" part will give you a sense of how the book goes about its task: Leverage, Mentors, Teams, Networks, Infinite Networks, Skills and Tools, Systems, Real Estate, Business. Again, Real Estate in 2009 ain't what it was in 2002 ... and, their *other* "wow" approach, The Internet, is far more crowded these days than back then, and a lot of what they suggest as techniques here would face a huge challenge "competing for eyeballs" in the current Web. However, as noted, the "broad strokes" here I believe still hold true, their "Enlightened Millionaire" philosophy is strong, and they do legitimately seem to be *trying* to drag the willing among us into the "millionaire club".

Of course, due to the caveats above, I can't give this a "wholehearted" recommendation, but I certainly found the book of value, and *especially* if you're planning on picking up the new book (*Cash In A Flash*), you'll want to check this out *first*. As I mentioned, I got this on Amazon via the new/used vendors, and paid three bucks (before shipping) for my copy ... you, however, at the moment have the ability to snag "Like New" copies for as little as a penny, as I see there are several available there for considerably less than I paid. So, if you think that spending four bucks (1¢ + $3.99 s/h) for some primo "visionary business coaching" is worth it to you, I'd say jump on this today.

Notes:

1. http://btripp-books.livejournal.com/84923.html
2. http://amzn.to/1VNcrxQ

Sunday, November 22, 2009[1]

What a bummer!

A few weeks back, somebody commenting on one of the posts in my main journal *strongly* encouraged my reading some George Carlin. Since I've been "coached" to *consider the serendipitous* for the job search and much associated with it, I decided to take up the suggestion and order in *three* of Carlin's books. All I can say after reading Brain Droppings[2] is that I'm glad i got them from Amazon's new/used vendors.

As regular readers of this space know, I've been spending a lot of time pumping my brain full of Intention, Positivity, Attraction and other Secret-esqe philosophies. In fact, one book (the classic The Science of Getting Rich[3], which I'm still quite enthusiastic about) counsels one to "not read any *other* philosophies" while working towards wealth. Well, this collection of Carlin's musings is just about as anti all that as is humanly possible. An earlier edition of myself would have found that quite amusing (heck, there's a section in here, Rules To Live By , which almost point-for-point goes down the list of things that the Secret people focus on, and presents a cynical and extremely negative version of them) in its complete dark mirroring of the fluff bunny movement. How'd he know? This book came out in 1997, so was penned nearly a decade before Byrne's book (you don't suppose *she* read this and was inspired to counter it?).

Frankly, I was unprepared for this to be any sort of a "challenging read", expecting to just blow through it and the others in a spare few hours. Instead, it was *a grind*, and surprisingly *unfunny*. While Carlin's work is certainly cerebral, picking apart language, looking at unacknowledged aspects of society, etc., I think it loses *a lot* when distilled down to simple text. Much of the punch to Carlin's humor is in the verbal *delivery*, and he's most effective when he can "mug along" with the jokes. Without the audio and video, the material here is *at best* "wry", but frequently giving the impression of "trying too hard" to get to some semblance of a punch line. I probably *chuckled* 2-3 times over the entire 258-page book (contrast that to the recent Kinky Friedman book[4] which had me LOL'ing every few pages).

The tone here, separate from Carlin's stagecraft, is uniformly bitter, hostile, non-constructively confrontational, fatalistic, and mean-spirited. Reading through the book was akin to having to take a long Greyhound bus ride stuck in a seat next to the most cantankerous, negative, and opinionated person you know. In the introduction to his *second* book, Carlin notes that this one did better than he'd anticipated. I'm surprised as well ... but it must have been as a new product by a cultural icon rather than on the strength of what's on the page. I used to joke that my poetry collections were written for those "too happy" people out there, Brain Droppings[5] comes across as being intended as a "cure" for those suffering from a surfeit of *positivity*. Needless to say, I'm very confused as to WHY the person (not a regular commentator in my journal) suggested that I read George Carlin's books ... I'm beginning to suspect that it was *intended* to sabotage whatever progress I've made "towards the light"!

As one might expect from the above, I am *not* recommending this, unless one wants to have it for a "historical" or "pop cultural" perspective. If one *does* feel a need to get a copy, I would recommend *not* spending the $27.95 that Amazon wants for a new copy, but pick up a "like new" copy for 1¢ (well, $4 with the $3.99 shipping, that's what I paid) from the used vendors!

Notes:

1. http://btripp-books.livejournal.com/85134.html
2. http://amzn.to/21FQCju
3. http://goo.gl/z4tXA4
4. http://btripp-books.livejournal.com/83076.html
5. http://amzn.to/21FQCju

Sunday, December 6, 2009[1]

Better ...

So, as I noted previously, I'm in the midst of reading three of George Carlin's books. I had certain "issues" with his previous one, Brain Droppings[2], and, in reading this, I'm guessing that many of *my* complaints about it were also eventually raised by others (perhaps his publisher), as this second book Napalm & Silly Putty[3] is far more "literary" and less "this is my stage show" than its predecessor. There were far fewer places in this where the material felt like it "needed" his timing and mugging to make it work.

One thing that I found surprising was that various bits from the previous book found their way in here. Of course, I'm hitting all three of these books in succession, so am far more likely to *notice* than the vast majority of folks reading them, and (barring some obsessive-compulsive filing/indexing system to keep track) it's certainly understandable how repeats *could* sneak in, given there being as many as 8 bits per page in a 250+ page collection. Anyway, these were not all over the place, but there were a half a dozen to a dozen that "jumped off the page" while reading this.

With the change of focus, I felt the book was far more amusing than its predecessor, with many well-constructed "riffs" on various topics ... one about "maniacs and crazy people" especially caught my fancy, with this particular chunk seeming worth sharing:

> ... you can't put them all away. You have to keep some of them around just for the entertainment. Like the guy who tells you the King of Sweden is using his gallbladder as a radio transmitter to send anti-Semitic lesbian meat loaf recipes to Marvin Hamlisch. A guy like that, you want to give him his own radio show.

That's still recognizably *Carlin*, but less a stage riff and more, a "story".

The book is also somewhat more systematically organized with blocks of related subject matter pulled together ("Cars And Driving", "Dog Moments", etc.), and the one- or two-liners grouped in "Short Takes" sections every 10-20 pages (and differentiated with a slight grey screen in the background). This also makes the book stand more as a "book".

Like the previous title, I picked this up from the Amazon new/used guys for a penny (plus shipping), but it does still seem to be in print ... frankly, I'm amazed that Amazon is charging full cover (and that's above twenty bucks each, the three Carlin books I got would have come in just under $75 if I hadn't gone with the new/used guys!) for these, but I'm sure there are folks out there who really get into this. Don't get me wrong, I'd been a fan of Carlin's, but I'd been a fan of his *act*, and the books, while bringing the *content* don't do so with the *sell* (voice inflection, rubber-faced mugging, etc.) which brought home the absurdities he was commenting on. While Napalm & Silly Putty[4] is *better* than its predecessor, I'm glad I was able to get it for just four bucks!

Notes:

1. http://btripp-books.livejournal.com/85446.html
2. http://btripp-books.livejournal.com/85134.html
3-4. http://amzn.to/1YdLiSD

Thursday, December 10, 2009[1]

Well, that's the third of three of these ...

So, this is the third of the three George Carlin books I picked up recently. Having read all three (I believe the fourth was posthumous) I'm pretty firmly of the opinion that Carlin is best preserved *in video* rather than on the page. While his wit and curiosity come through on paper, it's dimmed by the lack of vocal delivery and stagecraft which made his act so impactful. When Will Jesus Bring The Pork Chops?[2] is much like his second book, *Napalm & Silly Putty* in structure, with longer thematic sections being intermittently broken up by short bits. I'm not much of a "video guy", but the weakness of these collections has made me seriously consider picking up some of his video releases, as there's just enough here to remind one of his genius, but it's like a super-model in a parka ... the best parts just aren't on display!

Frankly, I had hoped from the title that this was going to be a significant broadside at organized religion, but (while there is this content, but no more so than in his previous books), this was not the case. I still am not sure *where* the title comes from, if it's a reference from a bit in the book, it certainly snuck past me, and I've not been able to place it in any other context. I would have been *much* happier with this if the majority of the material ran along the lines of this gem:

> *These anti-war demonstrators are really unimpressive people. They're against war? How groundbreaking: what a courageous stand. Listen, angry asshole, pick something difficult. Like religion. Why don't you get out on the street and start marching around against religion – something that's really harmful to mankind. War is simply nature's way or doing things; of keeping down the count. Religion is the problem. Get rid of religion and you've done the planet a favor. So how about getting out there next weekend and marching around with a sign that says HO HO HO! RELIGION MUST GO! Come on, protesters, show some balls.*

Of course, I like that because it slams both the Left and the Fundies all in one go ... and if the book were *all* that way, it would be an "instant classic" in my library and high on the list of my favorite books! Considering what a counter-cultural icon he was, it's very amusing to find him poking the "liberal cause" morons with sharp sticks. There was this brief jab that sums up the mental insufficiency of the "do-gooder" dingbats:

> *A lot of the people who worry about the safety of nuclear plants don't bother using their seat belts.*

... obviously pointing out that those sort of people aren't particularly good at *math*! I assume that it goes without saying that Carlin wasn't coming from the *other* camp either, but going for a place of free thought that was willing to say that the Emperors (and their lackeys) of both the left and right rarely had any clothes. This snippet is a great example:

> *I don't like ass kissers, flag wavers or team players. I like people who buck the system. I often warn kids: "Somewhere along the way, someone is going to tell you, 'There is no "I" in team.' What you should tell them is, 'Maybe not. But there is an "I" in independence, individuality and integrity.'"*

As was the case with the earlier volumes, When Will Jesus Bring The Pork Chops?[3] is still in print, and so should be available at your local brick-and-mortar book vendor ... Amazon has it a *full cover price* (!), so if you're looking for a new copy, you might do better in meatspace, however, "like new" copies can be had from the new/used guys for as little as a penny (four bucks with shipping), so that would certainly be my recommendation were you wanting to pick up copy of this!

Notes:

1. http://btripp-books.livejournal.com/85613.html
2-3. http://amzn.to/1YdKSeV

Sunday, December 13, 2009[1]

We're doomed ...

This is another book that I got from the LibraryThing[2] "Early Reviewer" program, which matches up books provided by publishers with L.T. users who have requested review copies, and whose libraries (via the mysterious workings of "The Algorithm") provide a "best fit" for the title in question. I have, unfortunately, been in and out of the job search so much, that I guess I have more "looking for work" books that most, so ended up getting Ron McGowan's How to Find Work in the 21st Century[3] from the October availabilities.

I have to say, I did not *like* this book. Unlike, say, Conor Cunneen's, there is no cheerleading, no sense that if you focus on the job hunt, and do certain things, it will turn out OK. Nope. This has the emotional delicacy of Alan Rickman's Severus Snape putting an over-reaching student "back in his place", and reading it has a bit of the feel of being berated and belittled by the author. This is, however, not to say that this is not a very *useful* book, only that one needs to approach it "steeled" against the onslaught.

Much of the discomfort the book inspires arises from the author's stance that the "traditional job" is, essentially, *dead* and that everybody needs to get used to scraping for what funds they may be able to eke out from a constantly fluctuating mix of contracting/temporary/freelance gigs. At one point, discussing "young people" coming into this dire new world, he evens says:

> They may also want the material benefits that come from having a permanent job: a house, a nice car, and a comfortable lifestyle.

They *may* want these things? Who *doesn't* want these things? Obviously, the implication is that *these are no longer options* ... no house, no "nice" car, no "comfortable" lifestyle. The emotional imagery take-away is of all of North America (the author is Canadian) living in a "Mad Max"-style dumpster-diving economy!

Needless to say, I don't *think* this is the authors specific intent, but he does paint a very depressing picture of a world where there are nearly no "real jobs" and everybody is having to scramble 24/7 for whatever projects they can find. Now, a lot of "speculative" books I read are based on similar dire forecasts, and so I'm used to taking a scenario like this on its own terms. Given the underlying "doomed economy" message, the *practical* parts of the book are quite focused and helpful. Again, this is delivered with all the sympathy of Snape, but the book is organized in various sections:

"How The Workplace Has Changed" which discusses the author's views of the economy and the job market, "What Exactly Do You Have To Offer" (go ahead, hear that in Rickman's voice) which rather coldly has you pick apart whatever skill sets you might have believed you possessed to find what *could* be "marketable" in the new economy, "How To Market Yourself" which gives a reasonably detailed "action plan" (however unsentimentally presented) to find those bits and pieces of work (one can, perhaps, *generalize* this to a "job search", but it's clear that the author thinks that's a "sucker bet" at this point), and "Getting Started" which maps out what one should be doing to "find work". The next portion of the book addresses college students, and teachers of grade- and highschool students (not that the Teachers Unions would ever let ANY of these "reforms" be implemented in the U.S., especially the "co-op education" he suggests which sound a bit like apprenticeships from colonial times!), with versions of the material in the previous chapters aimed at these audiences' skill levels. Finally, there is "Managing Your Career", with more doom-and-gloom about how most Baby Boomers and following generational groups are totally screwed.

Again, if you accept the author's dystopian premises, *all* this makes perfect sense and fits into a reasonably congruent whole, complete with forms, templates, quizzes, etc. (which are conveniently assembled on an included CD-ROM). He certainly provides a *lot* of good advice, such as this gem from his "networking" discussion:

> ... avoid typical networking events that are continually being promoted by amateurs and others with a vested interest in attracting uninformed but well-meaning employment seekers.

... which is about as straight-forward as you can get on the idea of how useful a room full of desperate unemployed people are likely to be for each other!

There are, however, not a few "mixed messages" in the book ... these two snippets stood out (as they were pretty much directly across from each other on facing pages) as an example of this:

> Be realistic in your expectations of finding work on the Internet. Richard Bolles ... suggests that the average person has only a 2 percent chance of finding work on the Internet.

> The Internet is increasingly becoming the media of choice for companies looking to hire people and for people who are looking for work.

... uh, if it's the "media of choice" that's a pretty sorry state if it's only providing a 2% success rate!

To get a sense of the "tone" of the book, here's how the future the author envisions is presented in the section for kids:

> Coming to terms with bad news doesn't come easily to us but it's in our own self-interest to face up to the reality of what is going on in the economy. Like it or not, we must face the fact that for years some governments, a significant portion of industry, and the public have been living beyond

> their means and now we have to pay the price for that. We've become a society that seems to be incapable of facing up to the harsh reality that good times don't last forever and that going through tough times is a part of the natural cycle of life and the economy. Losing your job or your home or your savings is very hard to deal with but deal with it we must just as our ancestors had to in their time. Nobody knows how long the economic downturn will last or how deep it will be but there are some changes we can make now to get us back on track.

I don't know about *you* but reading that makes me want to move out to the boonies and stock up on food, fuel, and firearms rather than trying to figure out the best way to, hat-in-hand, look for piecework from whatever companies aren't bankrupt!

I want to reiterate that the *practical* advice/instructions given in the book are *top notch* and I've found many things (such as his suggestions for "brochures", which is a "marketing concept" for my own job search which I'd started on, but needed more honing of the concept) which I'm able to apply myself. The caveats being that this is not a "friendly" book and it is ultimately based on a *very* bleak view of the future.

It appears that, despite being part of the "Early Reviewer" program, How to Find Work in the 21st Century[4] has been around for a bit, as this is noted as being the "fifth edition" (although the initial date in the publishing info seems to only be 2008). If you're a job seeker in "tender" emotional condition, this might not be the best book for you, but if you're looking at going for an alternative career path, outside the "traditional job" this would be a nearly indispensable guidebook for what you need to do to get yourself ready for a nice piece of business in the *Thunderdome*.

Notes:

1. http://btripp-books.livejournal.com/85828.html
2. http://btripp-books.com/
3-4. http://amzn.to/1OhIsaA

Saturday, December 19, 2009[1]
Not quite connecting ...

This is yet another dollar store find ... which is, for a change, not that much of a surprise. The Call of the Weird: Travels in American Subcultures[2] is a follow-up to a documentary series that author Louis Theroux shot for the BBC in the '90s. As those of you "following along at home" may have noticed, there is a definite trend of documentary-related books ending up at the dollar store not too long after their publication (this had its American release in 2007), and the current volume certainly seems to fall in line with that pattern!

In this case, however, the disconnect is fairly easy to nail down ... the theme of this book is the author following up with ten of his previous documentary subjects, a decade or so past when he had first tracked their "weird" lives, and if one hasn't *seen* those programs, one is coming to this book totally cold, and dependent on the author to set up the "why" of these folks being featured. Now, the "weird" of the title is probably not the best descriptor for the people involved. They *are* participants in various "non-mainstream" *American Subcultures*, but aren't particularly remarkable in and of themselves. Theroux uses individuals within these contexts as a window onto the particular industry/movement/profession but really spends most of the book reflecting on *his* reactions as an "outsider" (although he is of dual UK/US citizenship and has lived extensively in the States).

His premise here is that he might be able, in follow-up visits *without* a camera/production crew, get "closer" to his former documentary subjects, and so find deeper insights into their "subcultures". So, he ends up moving to Las Vegas, buying a car, and seeing who he can track down. In most cases, he is forced to concentrate more on peripheral individuals who may or may not *know* the original subjects, and not so much on those folks, who in a number of these proved to be somewhat elusive.

Each chapter is devoted to one of these "weird" people ... first a fellow who had been very big in "UFO circles" when Theroux was shooting his program, but who had "disappeared" from that scene; the author eventually tracks him down, but the bulk of this deals with *other* UFO enthusiasts, with a brief visit with the original subject at the end ... next there's a young guy who had been a budding porn star at the time of the BBC series, but who had also moved on, and was very hard to find; again, much connecting with folks in the industry, followed by a brief visit with the subject in his new "normal" life ... then there's the one "celebrity" of the bunch, Ike Turner, who Theroux had an abortive attempt at a documentary of a tour previously; this encounter likewise falls apart, leaving the author musing on issues of trust and control ... next was a story about a fellow who had followed Colonel Bo Gritz up into the mountains of Idaho, only to not have the apocalypse they were anticipating come to pass and slowly fade into less dramatic lifestyles ... this was followed by a swing through Nevada's legal brothel industry, in search of a particular "working girl" that he'd featured previously; not surprisingly, she was also very hard to track down, so this chapter deals with a lot of *other* people in that milieu with a brief denouement of contact ... his next subject was an Aryan Nations member, back when that group was news, but it wasn't by the time the author got around to writing the book, and the guy had lost most of his "oddness" ... in an strange (and perhaps cynical given how it plays to the preceding subject's views of minorities) juxtaposition, he follows this up with a visit to Mississippi and a small-time pimp/rapper that had featured in one of his TV segments, here he has better *access* but far less *contact* being no more able to fit into the subject's world than had the author hailed from Alpha Centauri ... which could well be where his next subject wished to be, as he was a survivor of the Heaven's Gate cult, who had been given permission to leave before their mass suicide; here too, much of the chapter is spent with *other* former members, but it does provide a very interesting look into a somewhat unique situation ... it's then back to Las Vegas for the next subject, a sleazy "millionaire seminar" scammer, Theroux's access to the subject was very limited, so this again deals mainly with "victims" of the scam, some still quite devoted to the program ... finally, he's back in neo-Nazi land, tracking down the girls (and their mom) of the hate-rock band "Prussian Blue" (you may have seen pics on the web of the cute blonde twins in their "Hitler smiley face" t-shirts), resulting in the author trying to probe the kids' devotion to their Mother's (and grandparents') political/racial stance, to the irritation/frustration of all involved.

While, as "slice of life" features, these are all *interesting enough* on their own, yet without the connection to the preceding documentaries to cause one to particularly *care* about the subjects, it's a pretty weak set of stories, more the sort of things that might be "filler" in a magazine that the core of a book.

As I noted, I got The Call of the Weird[3] (in hard cover) from the dollar store, however it does appear to still be in print in a paperback edition ... just in case you were anxious to run out and find a copy. The Amazon new/used guys have "like new" copies for two bucks (plus shipping), so you might consider that if you can't find a dollar store copy. Again, this was a mildly engaging collection of stories, but you'd either have to have been a fan of the BBC documentaries to really be into this enough to pay retail!

Notes:

1. http://btripp-books.livejournal.com/86237.html
2-3. http://amzn.to/1YdJPeS

QR code links
to the
on-line reviews:

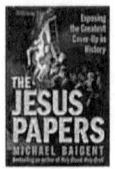

The Jesus Papers:
Exposing the Greatest Cover-Up in History
by
Michael Baigent

Flatland: A Romance of Many Dimensions
by
Edwin A. Abbot

Greece Before Homer:
Ancient Chronology and Mythology
by
John Forsdyke

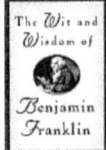

The Wit and Wisdom of Benjamin Franklin
by
Benjamin Franklin

Quality Management in the Nonprofit World:
Combining Compassion and Performance
to Meet Client Needs and Improve Finances
by
Larry W. Kennedy

The Starseed Dialogues:
Soul Searching the Universe
by
Patricia Cori

The Sion Revelation:
The Truth About the Guardians
of Christ's Sacred Bloodline
by
Lynn Picknett & Clive Prince

Buddha for Beginners
by
Stephen T. Asma

BTRIPP BOOKS - 2013   169

Secrets of the Widow's Son:
The Mysteries Surrounding the Sequel
to The Da Vinci Code
by
David A. Shugarts

Ticket To Ride:
Inside the Beatles' 1964 Tour that Changed the World
by
Larry Kane

The Cleft and Other Odd Tales
by
Gahan Wilson

For This Land: Writings on Religion in America
by
Vine Deloria, Jr.

The Kuan Yin Chronicles:
The Myths and Prophecies
of the Chinese Goddess of Compassion
by
Martin Palmer

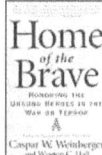

Home of the Brave:
Honoring the Unsung Heroes in the War on Terror
by
Caspar Weinberger & Wynton C. Hall

The Mars Mystery:
The Secret Connection Between Earth
and the Red Planet
by
Graham Hancock

The Garden of Heaven: Poems of Hafiz
by
Hafiz & Gertrude Bell

A Foreign Policy of Freedom:
Peace, Commerce, and Honest Friendship
by
Ron Paul

The Vast Right-Wing Conspiracy's
Dossier on Hillary Clinton
by
Amanda B. Carpenter

The Dalai Lama's Little Book of Inner Peace:
The Essential Life and Teachings
by
His Holiness the Dalai Lama

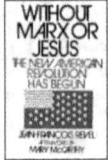

Without Marx or Jesus:
The New American Revolution Has Begun
by
Jean-François Revel

Fight Back:
Tackling Terrorism, Liddy Style
by
G. Gordon Liddy

Secrets of the Unified Field:
The Philadelphia Experiment, The Nazi Bell,
and the Discarded Theory
by
Joseph P. Farrell

Competitive Intelligence:
How to Gather Analyze and Use Information
to Move Your Business to the Top
by
Larry Kahaner

Masters of the Living Energy:
The Mystical World of the Q'ero of Peru
by
Joan Parisi Wilcox

Are We Alone?:
Philosophical Implications
Of The Discovery Of Extraterrestrial Life
by
Paul Davies

Anasazi:
Ancient People of the Rock
by
David Muench & Donald G. Pike

F5: Devastation, Survival,
and the Most Violent Tornado Outbreak
of the 20th Century
by
Mark Levine

Ning for Dummies
by
Manny Hernandez

Treasures of the Library of Congress
by
Charles A Goodrum

The Russian Version of the Second World War:
The History of the War As Taught to
Soviet Schoolchildren
by
Graham Lyons, Ed.

Views from the Real World: Early Talks Moscow,
Essentuki, Tiflis, Berlin, London, Paris, New York,
and Chicago as Recollected by His Pupils
by
G.I. Gurdjieff

The Republic
by
Plato

BTRIPP BOOKS - 2013   175

Religion In Practice
by
Swami Prabhavananda

Google AdSense for Dummies
by
Jerri Ledford

The Aquarian Gospel of Jesus the Christ
by
Levi H. Dowling

Understanding the Enneagram:
The Practical Guide to Personality Types
by
Don Richard Riso

 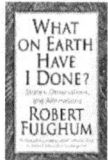

What On Earth Have I Done?:
Stories, Observations, and Affirmations
by
Robert Fulghum

Civilization One:
The World is Not as You Thought It Was
by
Christopher Knight & Alan Butler

The Woman with the Alabaster Jar:
Mary Magdalen and the Holy Grail
by
Margaret Starbird

The Holy Place:
Discovering the Eighth Wonder of the Ancient World
by
Henry Lincoln

BTRIPP BOOKS - 2013   177

Cosmic Jackpot:
Why Our Universe Is Just Right for Life
by
Paul Davies

The Path of the Pole
by
Charles Hapgood

The Passover Plot
by
Hugh J. Schonfield

What About the Big Stuff?:
Finding Strength and Moving Forward
When the Stakes Are High
by
Richard Carlson, Ph.D.

The Tipping Point:
How Little Things Can Make a Big Difference
by
Malcolm Gladwell

Biomimicry:
Innovation Inspired by Nature
by
Janine M. Benyus

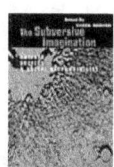

The Subversive Imagination:
Artists, Society & Social Responsibility
by
Carol Becker, Ed.

Love, Sex, Fear, Death:
The Inside Story of The Process Church
of the Final Judgment
by
Timothy Wyllie

QED:
The Strange Theory of Light and Matter
by
Richard P. Feynman

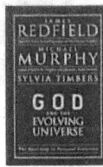

God and the Evolving Universe:
The Next Step in Personal Evolution
by
James Redfield, Michael Murphy & Sylvia Timbers

Never Again:
Securing America and Restoring Justice
by
John Ashcroft

Painting the Map Red:
The Fight to Create a Permanent
Republican Majority
by
Hugh Hewitt

Winning The Future:
A 21st Century Contract with America
by
Newt Gingrich

The Intention Experiment:
Using Your Thoughts
to Change Your Life and the World
by
Lynn McTaggart

The Jasons:
The Secret History of Science's Postwar Elite
by
Ann Finkbeiner

Almost Home:
A Correspondence with a Spiritual Teacher
by
Kevin Edwards (Prakash)

The Master:
Parables For Enlightenment
by
Kevin Edwards

Civilizations of the Indus Valley and Beyond
by
Sir Mortimer Wheeler

The Career Guide
for Creative and Unconventional People
by
Carol Eikleberry

The Riddle of the Pyramids
by
Kurt Mendelssohn

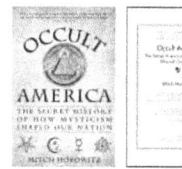

Occult America:
The Secret History
of How Mysticism Shaped Our Nation
by
Mitch Horowitz

The Presence of the Past:
Morphic Resonance and the Habits of Nature
by
Rupert Sheldrake

The Templars' Secret Island:
The Knights, The Priest, and The Treasure
by
Henry Lincoln & Erling Haagensen

SHEIFGAB the World:
8 Building Blocks to Successful Job Transition
by
Conor Cunneen

The Classic Tradition of Haiku
by
Faubion Bowers

The New Science of Getting Rich
by
Wallace D. Wattles

Principia Discordia
by
Gregory Hill (Malaclypse The Younger) &
Kerry Thornley (Omar Khayyam Ravenhurst)

Enchiridion
by
Epictetus

Cowboy Logic:
The Wit and Wisdom of
Kinky Friedman (and Some of His Friends)
by
Kinky Friedman

Beyond Ego:
Transpersonal Dimensions in Psychology
by
Roger N. Walsh, M.D., Ph.D
& Frances Vaughan, Ph.D

The Jesus Family Tomb:
The Discovery, the Investigation,
and the Evidence That Could Change History
by
Simcha Jacobovici & Charles Pellegrino

50 Ways to Thrive,
Putting the Sizzle Back Into Your Life:
A New Look at the Possibilities for Human Beings
by
Dr. Richard Talsky

The Sacred Geometry of Washington D.C.:
The Integrity And Power of the Original Design
by
Nicholas R. Mann

Freakonomics:
A Rogue Economist
Explores the Hidden Side of Everything
by
Steven D. Levitt & Stephen J. Dubner

Stepping Up:
Make Decisions that Matter
by
Timothy Dobbins

The One Minute Millionaire:
The Enlightened Way to Wealth
by
Mark Victor Hansen & Robert G. Allen

Brain Droppings
by
George Carlin

Napalm & Silly Putty
by
George Carlin

When Will Jesus Bring The Pork Chops?
by
George Carlin

How to Find Work in the 21st Century
by
Ron McGowan

The Call of the Weird:
Travels in American Subcultures
by
Louis Theroux

CONTENTS - ALPHABETICAL BY AUTHOR

Edwin A. Abbot — *Flatland* — page 4

John Ashcroft — *Never Again* — page 101

Stephen T. Asma — *Buddha for Beginners* — page 16

Michael Baigent — *The Jesus Papers* — page 1

Carol Becker — *The Subversive Imagination* — page 93

Gertrude Bell — *The Garden of Heaven* — page 32

Janine M. Benyus — *Biomimicry* — page 91

Faubion Bowers — *The Classic Tradition of Haiku* — page 131

George Carlin — *Brain Droppings* — page 156

George Carlin — *Napalm & Silly Putty* — page 158

George Carlin — *When Will Jesus Bring The Pork Chops?* — page 160

Richard Carlson, Ph.D. — *What About the Big Stuff?* — page 87

Amanda B. Carpenter — *The Vast Right-Wing Conspiracy's Dossier on Hillary Clinton* — page 36

Patricia Cori — *The Starseed Dialogues* — page 11

Conor Cunneen — *SHEIFGAB the World* — page 128

His Holiness the Dalai Lama — *The Dalai Lama's Little Book of Inner Peace* — page 38

Paul Davies — *Are We Alone?* — page 50

Paul Davies   page   81
                    Cosmic Jackpot

Vine Deloria, Jr.   page   24
                    For This Land

Timothy Dobbins   page 152
                    Stepping Up

Levi H. Dowling   page   69
          The Aquarian Gospel of Jesus the Christ

Kevin Edwards   page 111
                    Almost Home

Kevin Edwards   page 113
                    The Master

Carol Eikleberry   page 117
     The Career Guide for Creative and Unconventional People

Epictetus   page 138
                    Enchiridion

Joseph P. Farrell   page   44
               Secrets of the Unified Field

Richard P. Feynman   page   97
          QED: The Strange Theory of Light and Matter

Ann Finkbeiner   page 109
                    The Jasons

John Forsdyke   page   6
                 Greece Before Homer

Kinky Friedman   page 140
                    Cowboy Logic

Robert Fulghum   page   73
               What On Earth Have I Done?

Newt Gingrich   page 105
                   Winning The Future

Malcolm Gladwell   page   89
                   The Tipping Point

Charles A Goodrum   page   57
            Treasures of the Library of Congress

G. I. Gurdjieff   page   61
                 Views from the Real World

Graham Hancock *The Mars Mystery*	page	30
Mark Victor Hansen & Robert G. Allen *The One Minute Millionaire*	page	154
Charles Hapgood *The Path of the Pole*	page	83
Manny Hernandez *Ning for Dummies*	page	55
Hugh Hewitt *Painting the Map Red*	page	103
Mitch Horowitz *Occult America*	page	122
Simcha Jacobovici & Charles Pellegrino *The Jesus Family Tomb*	page	144
Larry Kahaner *Competitive Intelligence*	page	46
Larry Kane *Ticket To Ride*	page	20
Larry W. Kennedy *Quality Management in the Nonprofit World*	page	9
Christopher Knight & Alan Butler *Civilization One*	page	75
Jerri Ledford *Google AdSense for Dummies*	page	67
Mark Levine *F5*	page	53
Steven D. Levitt & Stephen J. Dubner *Freakonomics*	page	150
G. Gordon Liddy *Fight Back*	page	42
Henry Lincoln *The Holy Place*	page	79
Henry Lincoln & Erling Haagensen *The Templars' Secret Island*	page	126
Graham Lyons *The Russian Version of the Second World War*	page	59

Malaclypse the Younger page 136
Principia Discordia

Nicholas R. Mann page 148
The Sacred Geometry of Washington D.C.

Ron McGowan page 162
How to Find Work in the 21st Century

Lynn McTaggart page 107
The Intention Experiment

Kurt Mendelssohn page 119
The Riddle of the Pyramids

Martin Palmer, Jay Ramsay & Man-Ho Kwok page 26
The Kuan Yin Chronicles

Ron Paul page 34
A Foreign Policy of Freedom

Lynn Picknett & Clive Prince page 13
The Sion Revelation

Donald G. Pike & David Muench page 52
Anasazi

Plato page 63
The Republic

Swami Prabhavananda page 65
Religion In Practice

James Redfield, Michael Murphy & Sylvia Timbers page 99
God and the Evolving Universe

Jean-François Revel page 40
Without Marx or Jesus

Don Richard Riso page 71
Understanding the Enneagram

Hugh J. Schonfield page 85
The Passover Plot

Rupert Sheldrake page 124
The Presence of the Past

David A. Shugarts page 18
Secrets of the Widow's Son

Margaret Starbird page 77
The Woman with the Alabaster Jar

Dr. Richard Talsky						page	146
    50 Ways to Thrive

Louis Theroux						page	165
    The Call of the Weird

Roger N. Walsh, M.D., Ph.D. & Frances Vaughan, Ph.D.		page	142
    Beyond Ego

Wallace D. Wattles						page	133
    The New Science of Getting Rich

Caspar Weinberger						page	28
    Home of the Brave

Sir Mortimer Wheeler						page	115
    Civilizations of the Indus Valley and Beyond

Joan Parisi Wilcox						page	48
    Masters of the Living Energy

Gahan Wilson						page	22
    The Cleft and Other Odd Tales

S.M. Wu						page	8
    The Wit and Wisdom of Benjamin Franklin

Timothy Wyllie						page	94
    Love, Sex, Fear, Death

CONTENTS - ALPHABETICAL BY TITLE

50 Ways to Thrive
Dr. Richard Talsky   page 146

Almost Home
Kevin Edwards   page 111

Anasazi
Donald G. Pike & David Muench   page 52

The Aquarian Gospel of Jesus the Christ
Levi H. Dowling   page 69

Are We Alone?
Paul Davies   page 50

Beyond Ego
Roger N. Walsh, M.D., Ph.D. & Frances Vaughan, Ph.D.   page 142

Biomimicry
Janine M. Benyus   page 91

Brain Droppings
George Carlin   page 156

Buddha for Beginners
Stephen T. Asma   page 16

The Call of the Weird
Louis Theroux   page 165

The Career Guide for Creative and Unconventional People
Carol Eikleberry   page 117

Civilization One
Christopher Knight & Alan Butlerton   page 75

Civilizations of the Indus Valley and Beyond
Sir Mortimer Wheeler   page 115

The Classic Tradition of Haiku
Faubion Bowers   page 131

The Cleft and Other Odd Tales
Gahan Wilson   page 22

Competitive Intelligence
Larry Kahaner   page 46

Cosmic Jackpot
Paul Davies   page 81

Kinky Friedman   *Cowboy Logic*   page 140

The Dalai Lama's Little Book of Inner Peace
His Holiness the Dalai Lama   page 38

Enchiridion
Epictetus   page 138

F5
Mark Levine   page 53

Fight Back
G. Gordon Liddy   page 42

Flatland
Edwin A. Abbot   page 4

For This Land
Vine Deloria, Jr.   page 24

A Foreign Policy of Freedom
Ron Paul   page 34

Freakonomics
Steven D. Levitt & Stephen J. Dubner   page 150

The Garden of Heaven
Gertrude Bell   page 32

God and the Evolving Universe
James Redfield, Michael Murphy & Sylvia Timber   page 99

Google AdSense for Dummies
Jerri Ledford   page 67

Greece Before Homer
John Forsdyke   page 6

The Holy Place
Henry Lincoln   page 79

Home of the Brave
Caspar Weinberger   page 28

How to Find Work in the 21st Century
Ron McGowan   page 162

The Intention Experiment
Lynn McTaggart   page 107

The Jasons
Ann Finkbeiner   page 109

The Jesus Family Tomb
Simcha Jacobovici & Charles Pellegrino   page   144

The Jesus Papers
Michael Baigent   page   1

The Kuan Yin Chronicles
Martin Palmer, Jay Ramsay & Man-Ho Kwok   page   26

Love, Sex, Fear, Death
Timothy Wyllie   page   94

The Mars Mystery
Graham Hancock   page   30

The Master
Kevin Edwards   page   113

Masters of the Living Energy
Joan Parisi Wilcox   page   48

Napalm & Silly Putty
George Carlin   page   158

Never Again
John Ashcroft   page   101

The New Science of Getting Rich
Wallace D. Wattles   page   133

Ning for Dummies
Manny Hernandez   page   55

Occult America
Mitch Horowitz   page   122

The One Minute Millionaire
Mark Victor Hansen & Robert G. Allen   page   154

Painting the Map Red
Hugh Hewitt   page   103

The Passover Plot
Hugh J. Schonfield   page   85

The Path of the Pole
Charles Hapgood   page   83

The Presence of the Past
Rupert Sheldrake   page   124

Principia Discordia
Malaclypse the Younger   page   136

QED: The Strange Theory of Light and Matter
Richard P. Feynman   page   97

Quality Management in the Nonprofit World
Larry W. Kennedy   page   9

Religion In Practice
Swami Prabhavananda   page   65

The Republic
Plato   page   63

The Riddle of the Pyramids
Kurt Mendelssohn   page   119

The Russian Version of the Second World War
Graham Lyons   page   59

The Sacred Geometry of Washington D.C.
Nicholas R. Mann   page   148

Secrets of the Unified Field
Joseph P. Farrell   page   44

Secrets of the Widow's Son
David A. Shugarts   page   18

SHEIFGAB the World
Conor Cunneen   page   128

The Sion Revelation
Lynn Picknett & Clive Prince   page   13

The Starseed Dialogues
Patricia Cori   page   11

Stepping Up
Timothy Dobbins   page   152

The Subversive Imagination
Carol Becker   page   93

The Templars' Secret Island
Henry Lincoln & Erling Haagensen   page   126

Ticket To Ride
Larry Kane   page   20

The Tipping Point
Malcolm Gladwell   page   89

Treasures of the Library of Congress
Charles A Goodrum   page   57

Understanding the Enneagram
Don Richard Riso   page   71

The Vast Right-Wing Conspiracy's Dossier on Hillary Clinton
Amanda B. Carpenter   page   36

Views from the Real World
G. I. Gurdjieff   page   61

What About the Big Stuff?
Richard Carlson, Ph.D.   page   87

What On Earth Have I Done?
Robert Fulghum   page   73

When Will Jesus Bring The Pork Chops?
George Carlin   page 160

Winning The Future
Newt Gingrich   page 105

The Wit and Wisdom of Benjamin Franklin
S.M. Wu   page   8

Without Marx or Jesus
Jean-François Revel   page   40

The Woman with the Alabaster Jar
Margaret Starbird   page   77

www.ingramcontent.com/pod-product-compliance
Lightning Source LLC
Chambersburg PA
CBHW060515100426
42743CB00009B/1325